Sarum Chronicle

recent historical research on Salisbury & district

Issue 14: 2014

ISBN 978-0-9571692-5-8 ISSN: 1475-1844

How to contact us:
   To order a copy phone Ruth Newman on 01722 328922 or email ruth. tanglewood@btinternet.com
   For other titles in the *Sarum Studies* series and for back issues of *Sarum Chronicle* please contact Jane Howells on 01722 331426 or email as below.
   To submit material for consideration in future editions of *Sarum Chronicle* email Jane Howells at jane@sarum-editorial.co.uk with the words Sarum Chronicle in the subject line.

Editorial Team: John Chandler, John Elliott, Jane Howells, Andrew Minting, Ruth Newman, Margaret Smith

www.sarumchronicle.wordpress.com

Designed and typeset by John Elliott

Contents

Editorial

S*arum Chronicle* depends on its authors. Without the contributions from local historians of Salisbury and the surrounding area there would be no journal for you to read. Over the years we have published articles from people who have never seen their name in print before, and from those for whom this experience is a relative commonplace.

As editors we are always delighted to receive offers and suggestions for articles. Occasionally we have asked someone to consider writing for us, especially when there is a particular topic we want to include. *Very* occasionally we have politely turned down an offer, usually because the material is easily available elsewhere or because we felt it was not directly appropriate for this journal.

So it is pure chance that in this issue we have a number of articles about art and artists. They are very different, but each in its own way demonstrates how an aesthetic element is to be found within the historian's area of interest. We hope you will discover some new artists and perhaps different ways of seeing your locality. For this special issue we are most grateful for the support of Mr Fred Uhde, who would be delighted to hear from any reader who has more ideas about his painting.

The diversity of the rest of the contents of SC14 confirms our determination *not* to plan for themed issues. One of the strong messages we have received from readers is that they particularly enjoy the diversity of local history represented in our publication; revealed in comments such as 'I bought this copy because of the article about X, and then unexpectedly found those on W, Y and Z equally enthralling'.

We would like to extend our thanks to Sue Johnson for her commitment to the journal since it began, and particularly for her meticulous copy-editing, and to David Richards who has been a thoughtful and enthusiastic member of the team; both will be sorely missed. A warm welcome goes to Andrew Minting who has joined us.

The viewpoint of the painting, on OS map 1901

A Later 18th Century Painting of Salisbury from the South-West

Tim Tatton-Brown with Jane Howells

On 9 July 1986, a fine, large, panoramic 18th century oil painting of Salisbury from the south-west was sold at Sotheby's for £44,000. It was sold 'by order of His Grace the Duke of Hamilton and Brandon' and for provenance, the catalogue[1] says 'Possibly James, 2nd Lord Fife, who built up a large collection of paintings in the 1770s', and 'By descent to HRH The Princess Royal, Duchess of Fife, at Moncoffer, Banffshire'. The catalogue

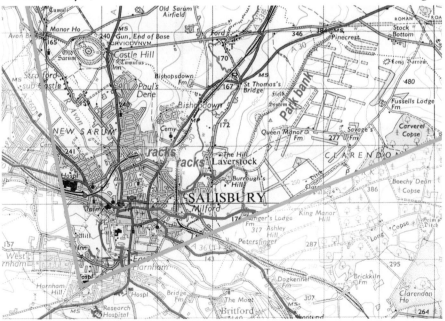

Features in the painting, on OS map 1950s

calls the painting 'an extensive view of Salisbury' and says it is of the English School, *circa* 1780. It gives the dimensions of the picture as 89 by 240 cm (35 by 94.5 inches).[2]

The American purchaser of the painting, Mr Frederick Uhde of Chicago, applied for an export licence, and after the Department of Trade and Industry's Expert Advisor objected (under the so-called 'Waverley criteria'), a hearing of the Reviewing Committee took place in November 1986.[3] It 'considered that the painting merited retention', and recommended 'that if, within five months, a public collection in this country offered to purchase the painting …. an export licence should not be issued'. No such offer was made, and the licence was duly granted. The painting then went to the USA, but in 2003 Mr Uhde came to live in London, and brought it with him.

This paper examines, in some detail, Salisbury in the later 18th century as seen in this painting. Buildings and other landmarks enable the viewer to identify the position of the painter, and the layout of the city within its landscape. There are also places that are unseen, either hidden behind other structures, or off the canvas to either side, that could be significant in discussing who might have commissioned the painting. That question is addressed in the concluding section of the paper. Some influential families

A view of Salisbury from Harnham Hill in the 18th century (Fred and Kathryn Uhde). Unless otherwise stated illustrations are details from this painting.

Stukeley's view from Harnham Hill, 1723 engraving

within the wider region, and then possible citizens of Salisbury itself, with the means and the interest in commissioning such a substantial and impressive work are suggested. In between, briefly, two possible artists are suggested but this issue is not developed here.

The painting itself is oil-on-canvas of exceptional size (about 3 feet high by 8 feet long) which shows the whole of Salisbury, and the surrounding area to the north and east, viewed from the top of Harnham Hill. Pride of place goes to Salisbury Cathedral just right of centre, and the familiar form of Old Sarum is on the skyline to the left. On the right hand side there are the sunlit western downs of Clarendon Park, with faint traces of a double rainbow. In the foreground a whole series of meadows and buildings can be seen, from West Harnham on the extreme left, through Fisherton and

Harnham Bridge (detail)

Salisbury to Ayleswade Bridge on the far right. The river Avon and parts of the Cathedral Close are prominent, as are various church towers, and some of the larger buildings. Behind the city and cathedral, on the hillsides to the right and left can also be seen long horizontal white lines, representing the tentering racks, where cloth was dried and stretched.[4] The most prominent hill on the skyline in the centre of the painting is probably Sidbury Hill, 735 ft above sea-level, and some 14.5 miles north-east of Salisbury. To its right, and also just standing out on the horizon (above the tower of St. Edmund's church) is perhaps Beacon Hill, near Bulford which is 668 ft. Some two thirds of the upper part of the painting are taken up with the sky, which is stormy, and contains some large cumulo-nimbus clouds. On the ground, the left hand side is mostly shown in shade, while the city and neighbouring meadows are shown in sunlight, with the sun coming from the west. This shows the time as afternoon, or late afternoon in the summer.

The painting itself must have been done from near the top of Harnham Hill, just south-west of Salisbury, a view that had already been depicted by William Stukeley in 1723. By using lines of sight on the various prominent buildings depicted, one can suggest that the artist's viewpoint was somewhere between the two highest points on the east and west ends of Harnham Hill at about 350 feet above sea-level.[5] The exact spot is hard to calculate because of many later trees, but it must be in the western part of the later Harnham Folly.

Looking in more detail at the buildings and landscape features depicted in the painting, it is possible to pick out key churches and houses. The draughtsmanship is somewhat inexact, and in places the perspective and scale of some of the buildings shown is muddled. One assumes that the view (or views) from the top of Harnham Hill were sketched, and then the oil painting was made, at a later date, in a studio. It may, of course, have been the intention of the artist to create a dramatic landscape based on what he had seen, rather than to make a precise representation of the view. Individual buildings would in that case be subsidiary to the overall effect.

Starting at the extreme right hand end of the picture, the most obvious feature that stands out is Harnham (or Ayleswade) Bridge. Four main arches are depicted, with the wide expanse of the river Avon in front. The Avon is more roughly shown moving away to the right, beyond the Bridge.[6] Unfortunately, almost nothing is shown of the buildings immediately beyond and south of the bridge, which had become known as East Harnham. They are, however, shown at the bottom of William Naish's early 18th century map of Salisbury, as are the beginning of the 'Road to Exeter' and the 'Road to Christ Church'.[7] The 'Road to Exeter' had recently been made a Turnpike Road,[8] and its steep course up Harnham Hill must have been just behind the artist. When John Constable sketched the view of Salisbury Cathedral from near the top of Harnham Hill in 1811, he was a little further south, and he does show the road coming up the hill, with behind it Ayleswade Bridge

St Martin's church, road to Clarendon, tenter racks (detail)

and the spire of St Martin's church.[9] Constable also sketched, in 1821, a similar view of the cathedral from further down the hill, near the main road from East to West Harnham.[10] Another view, done in 1827, from the same general area, by George Fennel Robson (1788-1833) shows the cathedral from the south-west, flanked by the churches of St Thomas and St Edmund (left) and St Martin (right).[11] It also shows grazing sheep in the foreground on the edge of the water meadows, and grazing sheep are also apparent in the bottom right hand corner of the present picture.

Ayleswade Bridge, a fine stone-arched bridge, was made in two sections in about 1240, the northern section of three arches (not shown in the picture) separated from the south-western section of six arches by a small island.[12] The artist only shows four of the six arches probably because the outer arches were concealed by the banks from his viewpoint. The bridge was widened and given new parapets in 1774, perhaps just after the painting was made. Two buildings are shown behind the left-hand end of the bridge; that on the right is perhaps the former 13th century chapel of St John (by then a house), while the building immediately adjacent to it on the left, may be the house opposite the chapel on the west side of the bridge.[13] Equally this gabled building, and the two structures to the left of it, may all belong to the Hospital of St Nicholas.[14] The draughtsmanship here is not sufficiently accurate for this to be certain. However, the road in front of these buildings is clearly Harnham Road, leading north from the bridge, which is then obscured on the left (west) by a small house and a wall (and trees) running west from the road. The wall then turns north, and behind it are a collection of buildings that must be on the De Vaux College site. Once again, the vague depiction of the buildings does not allow a detailed analysis of them, but they must contain the main later 13th century building of the College, which was depicted by Buckler, Constable and others, until its heavy restoration in the early 19th century.[15]

Behind this complex is a dense area of trees with beyond this another group of buildings with, on their right-hand side, the sun-lit west wall and tower and spire of St Martin's church, again not drawn exactly. Beyond the church on the right, a section of the old road to Southampton[16] can be seen, with behind it, the tree-covered boundary ditch and bank of Clarendon Park. West of the houses on the left side of St Martin's church is the curving road up Milford Hill. This leads on to Milford and the gateway into Clarendon Park at Ranger's Farm. To the left of this road is another area of buildings and trees in the upper part of the city, with open down land around Weeping Cross (now St Mark's roundabout) beyond. Immediately behind this, the long horizontal cloth drying racks are depicted, as mentioned above. The tree-covered bank and ditch of Clarendon Park is seen again behind the racks near Laverstock Hill.

Beneath all this, in the lower part of the picture, is the extreme south-west corner of the Cathedral Close, with a noticeable red-brick building. This must be the South Canonry which was to be almost totally rebuilt in 1890, but before then it was always an important and large canon's house.[17] The east front, however, still dates from the mid–18th century, when Canon Moss (1746-86) rebuilt it. The red-brick west wall shown in the picture is therefore probably very new.[18] To the north of the South Canonry a large open 'mead' can be seen on Naish's map, well shown in this picture, with the double tree-lined southern end of the West Walk in the Close on its east side. These trees, perhaps elms, were said to be planted in the mid-17th century,[19] so they were quite mature by the time of the picture. The other building among the trees is perhaps No 71a The Close, which was apparently at this time a stable building. It has a red-brick west wall,[20] but most of the rest of the building is still made of medieval masonry. To the right of the South Canonry two (or three) 'white' buildings can be seen, which must be Nos 72-73 The Close, rebuilt earlier in the 18th century, one as a lay vicar's house for the Revd John Talman in about 1754.[21] On its east side these houses adjoin the Harnham or South gate, and this can just be seen in the picture, with the masonry wall of the Close running away to the right. To the left of the buildings, many trees are shown, most of which must lie within the grounds of the bishop's palace. Because of the

St Thomas's, St Edmund's, College, bell-tower, Myles Place (detail)

tree cover, only the tops of the buildings of the bishop's palace can be seen, with most noticeably what is probably the south and west sides of the large later 15th century tower-porch, with its stair-turret and separate bell-cote.[22] They are roughly shown in grey and white paint. The bishop at this time was probably either the very elderly John Thomas (1761-6) or John Hume (1766-82). There is a useful undated plan of the bishop's grounds, which was perhaps made in 1783-4 for the next bishop, Shute Barrington (1782-91).[23] It shows all the details of the garden very clearly with large belts of trees along the western boundary, which must be the trees in the painting, running from near the chapter house to the area behind the Harnham gate. Above them, and the roofs of the palace,[24] houses in the town to the right (east) of the cathedral are seen. None can be individually identified, but they must lie in the chequers to the south-east of the marketplace.

The cathedral forms the centrepiece of the whole painting, though again this is not depicted with painstaking accuracy. For comparison, a fine late-17th century engraving, 'The South West Prospect of Salisbury Cathedral' by Robert Thacker provides a well-defined rendering.[25] Little has changed to the appearance of the south-west side of the cathedral in the last 250 years, but a few features are worth noticing. In Thacker's engraving, the very large mid-15th century library and lecture room building is shown covering the whole of the eastern range of the cloisters. In the picture, it is shown as it is today, a much shorter building. This is because the Dean and Chapter had decided, in late November 1758, that the southern part of the library building should be taken down, and this was probably done soon afterwards.[26] So this picture cannot have been painted until 1759, at the earliest. The neighbouring chapter house is shown with now vanished

Boat and gardens (detail)

crenellations on its south-western parapets, but these were only removed in the 1855-6 restoration of the building by Henry Clutton.[27]

Immediately in front of the cathedral, shown just below the cloister outer walls, are the roofs and upper parts of the buildings of the canons' houses called Leadenhall and the Walton Canonry.[28] None of these is clearly shown, but the next house to the north, Myles Place, which stands out above its neighbours, is carefully painted. It was built by, and for, William Swanton between1718 and 1722 as a four-storied mansion, and was lavishly decorated in the latest style.[29] Between 1744 and his death in 1778, it was leased by Dr Henry Hele, who became one of the first supervisory physicians of the new Salisbury General Infirmary (see below).

Almost directly above Myles Place can be seen the detached cathedral bell-tower, without its huge timber-framed upper section and spire.[30] The top belfry section is covered by a low-pitched pyramidal roof, painted red to show tiles. This roof must have been made in the year or so following another set of orders, given at the cathedral chapter meeting on 25 November 1758.[31] Here we read that the Spire and Tower on the belfry was to 'be forthwith taken down', and

> that the Masters of the ffabrick be desired to consider and take advice about a plan for finishing and complating the Belfry in a neat and proper manner when the Spire and Tower thereof shall be taken down.

These orders were countersigned by the bishop on 18 December 1758, so it is very likely that the work was carried out by the Clerk-of-Works, Edmund Lush in 1759 or not long after,[32] and that this painting cannot have been made until after the work was completed.

Immediately to the left of the bell-tower in the painting is a group of mature trees, which must be in the north-western corner of the cathedral churchyard. Below and left from Myles Place and these trees, are the other large houses and their outbuildings in the north-west part of the Close, though it is not easy to identify individual houses like the King's House, Deanery, North Canonry, Arundells, etc. Each had a large garden running down to the river, and one (the North Canonry) still has a large summer house on the river front, that was originally built for Arundells in the earlier 18th century.[33] The summer houses shown in the painting on the riverside are presumably others that were subsequently demolished. It is also worth noting here the group of figures in a boat with a small mast (and pennant) rowing northwards up the Avon near the garden of the King's House. To the left of this, the river curves round to the right off the large garden of the

View of Salisbury from Harnham Hill, Wiltshire, with Harvesters in the Foreground. George Cole 1810-1883 (circle of), (with permission © Salisbury City Council)

Deanery. Many trees and other vegetation in the spacious gardens (now, alas, filled with many later 20th century buildings) are casually depicted.

Left of the bell-tower and above the trees, the roofs of buildings are shown which end on the left with the tower (rebuilt 1653-6) and roof of St Edmund's church.[34] To the right of this is a turret and some other roofs which are probably part of St. Edmund's College (usually known as 'The College' at this time), 'the largest and handsomest private house in the town', to quote the Royal Commission on Historical Monuments.[35] It is a pity that this building is not more carefully shown, as exactly at this time, in the mid-18th century, the magnificent south front, that still exists today, was being refaced in a very handsome way by the Wyndham family. Behind these buildings, both to the right and left of St Edmund's tower, are shown more cloth-drying racks, as horizontal white lines, above where the railway tunnel was later built at the southern end of Bishopdown.

The next church tower to the left of St Edmund's is that of St Thomas's, correctly shown with its pointed lead roof, just sticking up above the parapet.[36] The west end of St Thomas's church is seen (among red roofs and chimneys) running west from the tower. To the right of St Thomas's church is the market place, but nothing of this, or of its associated buildings (Guildhall etc) is shown in the painting. One more prominent three-storied building appears in the middle ground between the two church towers. This

has a hipped roof, and a row of smaller projecting hip-roofs, and it appears to lie between the many tiled roofs and chimneys of the town behind it, and the larger roofs of the houses of the Close in front. It could be the still surviving new south range of the Workhouse (now Church House), which was built in 1728 as an enlargement to the fine 15th century townhouse in Crane Street, which became the Workhouse and Bridewell in 1634.[37] An alternative identification of this building is Mompesson House, on the north side of Choristers' Green, which had been rebuilt in 1701. It is in approximately the right location, if a little far to the west, and the depiction is no more inaccurate, in terms of numbers of windows, shape of roof, chimneys and so on, than Myles Place. The trees drawn to the right of the building are probably on the south side of 'The Green' in Choristers' Square.[38]

Not far to the north of the Workhouse, and just over Fisherton bridge in Fisherton Street, a fine new five-storied Infirmary was built for the City between 1768 and 1770 (it opened in 1771).[39] This building is clearly *not* shown in the painting (it would have stood out above the other roofs, to the west of St Thomas's church) suggesting that the picture was done before 1770 at the latest, when this building was nearing completion. It can be clearly seen in, for example, 'View of Salisbury from Harnham Hill, Wiltshire, with Harvesters in the foreground', circle of George Cole (1810-1883).[40]

Many other buildings in Salisbury are shown to the left of St Thomas's church, but none can be identified. The line of buildings then thins out above the curve in the river Avon and continues further to the left (west) until

Old Sarum, Old Castle Inn, St Clement's Fisherton (detail)

St Clement's Church, Fisherton Anger

Old Sarum

Old Castle Inn

St Thomas Church

Parsonage Farm, West Harnham

River Avon

River Nadder

St Edmund's
Church

St Edmund's
College

Cathedral
Bell-Tower

Road to
Clarendon

St Martin's
Church

Clarendon
Park

Myles
Place

South
Canonry

Ayleswade Bridge,
East Harnham

Salisbury
Cathedral

Parsonage Farm W Harnham (detail)

they reach a group of buildings around the tower of St Clement's church, Fisherton Anger.[41] The narrower line of buildings must be Fisherton Street, and beneath them is a line of trees, and the open space of the Harnham water meadows, but with no detail shown. Around the tower of Fisherton Anger church, the slightly larger buildings are those in the old village of Fisherton, including possibly Fisherton Mill to the left, and perhaps the Rectory to the right of the church.[42]

The Old Parsonage (Parsonage farm house) 2012 (photo Jane Howells)

Swans etc (detail)

Above Fisherton, the well-known form of Old Sarum has little detail, though the inner, and higher, banks around the castle stand out well above the outer ramparts. On its right hand flank, however, there is a prominent building with, curving around it, the traces of a main road. This must be what is now Castle Road, the main Turnpike leading north out of Salisbury, which passes around the east side of Old Sarum. The building is the Old Castle Inn, just south-east of the main east entrance to Old Sarum. This old inn was enlarged in the 18th century.[43] Immediately to the left of the building is a feature that may be the infamous Parliament Tree, where Members of Parliament were elected for the Rotten Borough until the 1832 Great Reform Act.[44] The Manor was owned by the Pitt family in the 18th century, and William Pitt the elder was MP for Old Sarum between 1734 and 1747.[45]

The extreme left hand end of the picture only contains a vague representation of fields, trees and hedgerows of the countryside west of Salisbury and north and south of Fisherton. In the bottom left hand corner, however, there is a group of buildings, which must be Parsonage Farm on the south-east side of the village of West Harnham.[46] Smoke is shown coming out of one of the chimneys and trees are painted quite carefully behind the buildings. The rest of the village including the church and large mill must be just out of the picture to the left. It is slightly surprising that they were not included.

The whole of the foreground of the picture shows the Harnham water meadows with lines of trees and a few hedges. The western branch of the river Nadder can be glimpsed at the very bottom of the picture with a pair of swans on the water, disproportionately prominent. Above them and to the left is perhaps a haystack, by a hedgerow. A few sheep appear near the swans, while to the left of the river bend there seems to be a flock of sheep with two cows (or perhaps horses?) to their left. The Harnham Slope and the road that runs between East and West Harnham are just off the bottom of the picture, and the whole of this area is now built up with 20th century houses. Harnham Slope, the steep north side of Harnham Hill has, in the last half century or so, become covered with scrubby trees, which now totally obscure the view in the picture. This is despite the fact that Bishop John Wordsworth (1885-1911) bought an area of ground on the north slope of the hill (which he called Harnwood) and made a fine pedestrian 'Walk' along the edge of it, which he presented to the City. There is a good (1905) photograph of the view from the top of Harnham Hill, before the trees grew up in *Mates Illustrated Guide*. It shows in the foreground the church of All Saints, built in 1854.[47]

As we have seen, this picture was almost certainly painted in the 1760s, but sadly, neither the artist, nor his patron, are known.

The artist

Whoever painted this view of Salisbury must have committed considerable time and energy to the task. It would have been created in his studio from sketches made in the field, and probably required several, if not many, visits to the site. The process of execution of a work of this size demanded resources of equipment and materials, and perhaps also assistance. Unless his patron was a generous and prompt paymaster, all this suggests the artist was someone with an established position, of some reputation, who could command sufficient trade credit.

It has been suggested that the artist of the painting may have been John Inigo Richards (1730/31 – 1810), a landscape and scene-painter, and founder member of the Royal Academy (he was also its Secretary from 1788 to his death).[48] There are certainly some elements of his style in the Salisbury picture, and it is worth noting that he painted a distant view of Wakefield that has some similarities.[49] However, many of Richards' paintings have carefully depicted figures in them, which the Salisbury one does not, so it is difficult to compare this to his other known work.[50] Richards is said to have visited Salisbury, and produced a watercolour of the cathedral belfry possibly in 1768.[51]

An alternative suggestion is that the artist might have been John Wootton (1681/2-1764). If so, this painting would have been accomplished at the very end of his long life, a considerable undertaking at such a time. A very versatile artist, Wootton was known for his landscape and sporting scenes, and did produce 'tapestry-size hunting pieces'.[52] He worked for the Duke of Beaufort who had a hunting lodge at Netheravon, north of Salisbury on the Plain. Recent authoritative comment, however, suggests the painting is 'not typical' for Wootton.[53]

The owners of the painting and possible people who might have commissioned it

Although eighteenth century artists did produce paintings for exhibition in anticipation of finding a subsequent purchaser, it is perhaps unlikely that that was the case for this particular work. Its exceptional size and specialised subject suggest it was commissioned by a wealthy collector, and probably someone with an interest in and/or a connection to the view of Salisbury that it depicts. In the next section of this paper some possible candidates are discussed.

As stated above, when the painting was auctioned at Sotheby's in 1986, it was put into the sale by the 15th Duke of Hamilton (and 12th Duke of Brandon). That much is known for certain. Given the wording on the 1986 Sotheby's catalogue it would seem the painting was acquired by the Duke of Hamilton after 1931, but that does not mean there was no Hamilton interest in it at an earlier date.

There are but slender links between the Dukes of Hamilton and Salisbury. The manor of Milford was leased to Alderman William Beckford in 1748, renewed to his son William in 1782 and 1832. Six years later it was assigned to *his* son-in-law Alexander, 10th Duke of Hamilton (d 1852), whose son William the 11th Duke sold the interest to the Ecclesiastical Commissioners in 1860.[54] William Beckford at Fonthill had a large and splendid art collection, but not of a style that would include this view from Harnham Hill. His younger daughter Susanna married Alexander Hamilton the 10th Duke who developed his own collections of paintings and other objects, much of which was dispersed in the 1880s, and later at further sales in the early 20th century. It is just possible that in the unlikely event this painting had been commissioned (or bought) by Beckford, it went with Susanna on her marriage. It does not appear in the catalogue of the 1823 'Fonthill Sale' at which Beckford's collection was largely bought back by himself and his son-in-law. And it has been noted that Milford itself is out of sight in the painting.

A little more likely is some connection with the Poore family. Although their main seat was further north in Wiltshire, Major Robert Poore (1834-1918) lived at Old Lodge, Winterslow. His eldest son Brigadier-General Robert Montagu Poore married Lady Flora Maria Ida Hamilton, and his youngest daughter Nina Mary Benita Poore married Alfred Douglas Douglas-Hamilton the 13th Duke (so two children married into the Hamilton family, brother and sister married sister and brother). The 13th Duke bought 'Ferne' a large house and estate west of Salisbury in 1915 (he died there in 1940), and he may have acquired the painting in the early 20th century.

On the reverse of the painting is a label stating 'from the collection of the late Princess Royal, Duchess of Fife, Montcoffer, Scotland'. Louise (1867-1931) was the third child and eldest daughter of the Prince and Princess of Wales who would become Edward VII and Queen Alexandra. In 1889 she married Alexander Duff, 6th Earl of Fife, who was made a duke by Queen Victoria. The Duchess lived a quiet country life; she was interested in music and photography, and her favourite sport was fishing. She was created Princess Royal by her father in 1905. The Duke and Duchess of Fife left their previous Scottish home, Duff House, in 1906[55] and moved to Montcoffer which was said to be 'furnished from Duff House'.[56] They also had a home in Brighton as well as a London house.

The family travelled to Egypt at the end of 1911 on board the liner *Delhi*. The ship ran aground, and the lifeboat carrying the royal party to safety capsized. They were all rescued and continued their journey to Tangier, Cairo and Khartoum. But tragedy struck when the Duke caught a chill that developed into pleurisy and he died in January 1912.[57]

The Princess Royal died in January 1931 and the contents of her house were sold. It was reported that there had been earlier dispersals of her property that included pictures, in July 1924 and December 1931.[58] This painting does not appear in the catalogues of either of these sales, nor in those of June 1925 or November 1926.[59]

The major landowners of the district around the city of Salisbury were the Earl of Pembroke at Wilton House and the Earl of Radnor at Longford Castle. Both houses have magnificent art collections of international repute. At the time it is thought this painting was created, army officer Henry Herbert was 10th Earl of Pembroke (1734-1794). His father the 9th Earl (1693-1750) has been described as a 'great patron of eighteenth-century art'[60] but was known particularly as an architect. The 10th Earl became an authority on the breaking of horses for the cavalry, and built the indoor riding school at Wilton. His estate does not feature directly in the painting, and there is no clear reason why he would want a view of Salisbury from Harnham Hill.

At Longford there was someone who might have commissioned the painting, William Bouverie, 2nd Viscount Folkestone (1724-76), who added 'Pleydell' to his name, after his marriage. He was MP for Salisbury from 1747-61, when he succeeded his father, and entered the House of Lords. In 1765, he was created the first Earl of Radnor, and at this time he owned much of the land on and around Harnham Hill, including the high ground from which the painting was done. He may also have first created the oval-shaped belt of trees on top of the hill, which was called Harnham Folly,[61] and through which the Blandford and Exeter road passed. So this picture could have been painted by an unknown local artist for the first Earl of Radnor, soon after he entered the House of Lords, as a reminder of his time as Salisbury MP. In surviving catalogues of the Longford art collection there is no item with a description matching this picture.[62]

Also in the vicinity, at Clarendon Park, Peter Bathurst had inherited the estate from his father, Peter, in 1748. The Bathursts had bought the estate from the Hydes in 1707 for £24,000, although the Hydes retained the title of Earls of Clarendon. Peter senior was MP for Salisbury between 1734 and 1741. He was responsible for the early 18th century construction of the house that forms the centrepiece of Clarendon Park today. Both Peter Bathursts used the estate to raise money; between 1754 and 1773 for example a debt of £9,000 was secured on the land by a series of mortgages, 'to finance family, political and social ends'.[63] Might it serve a social objective to spend on a splendid painting which stretches from Clarendon estate under a double rainbow across the neighbouring cathedral city? On the other hand, if funds were needed for the estate this would seem an unnecessarily frivolous purchase.[64]

Mawarden Court, Stratford-sub-Castle, was one of the homes of the Pitt family. Thomas Pitt (1653 – 1722) purchased the estate of Old Sarum in 1691 and it remained with them, giving them power over who represented the 'rotten borough' in Parliament until 1804. His great-grandson, another Thomas Pitt (1737-1793) held the seat from 1761 to 1768. His political career was closely enmeshed with those of his uncle ('Pitt the Elder') and cousin ('Pitt the Younger'). When the latter became Prime Minister, Thomas Pitt was offered a peerage and became 1ˢᵗ Baron Camelford in 1784. Known throughout his life for his 'deep and informed interest in the arts', Thomas Pitt had a house at Twickenham that was dubbed 'Palazzo Pitti'. One of his neighbours was Horace Walpole, and amongst his friends were the artist Angelica Kauffmann and architect John Soane.[65] The long and close association of the Pitts and Old Sarum, the castle's clear portrayal, with possibly the 'Parliament Tree', in the painting makes Lord Camelford another candidate for patron of this painting.

Somewhat more distant is St Giles House, at Wimborne St Giles, 15 miles southwest of Salisbury. This is the home of the Earls of Shaftesbury. Anthony Ashley-Cooper (1711 – 1771) the 4th Earl was married to Mary Pleydell-Bouverie, the sister of the 1st Earl of Radnor (see above). The present house was begun in the mid- 17th century, and a century later the 4th Earl developed it to suit the fashions of the time, adding two wings and expanding the contents with fine furniture and paintings. He had the surrounding park landscaped including a serpentine lake, a cascade and a grotto.[66] The 5th Earl's wife was Barbara Webb from Odstock House, even closer to Salisbury, but their wedding did not take place until 1786.

Salisbury residents

Within Salisbury, in the Close and other large houses in the town, were prominent citizens who might have had an interest in this painting. Whether any had the means or the inclination to be involved is perhaps even more speculative than the families and individuals already considered, but possible candidates are discussed in the next section of this paper.

Along the West walk, with gardens backing on to the river so included in the painting, are (from left to right) the South Canonry, Leadenhall, Walton Canonry, Myles Place, the Kings House, and others beyond to the north. Those named are not all very clearly drawn, but they can be identified by their location and some features of their building shape.

The South Canonry was occupied from 1746 to 1786 by Canon Moss who carried out some alterations to the building, but neither he nor the Eyre family who were there before and after Canon Moss's residence are known to have a particular interest in art, nor perhaps the means to undertake a commission such as this.[67]

It is unclear who resided at Leadenhall in the 1760s, though there had been considerable re-building earlier in the century. From 1772 the lease at Leadenhall was held by Canon Precentor Nathaniel Hume, Master of St Nicholas's Hospital, and brother to the Bishop Dr John Hume (Bishop 1766 to 1782). The Humes were a wealthy family related to the Marchmonts, who had a geographical connection with the Hamiltons in the Scottish borders. A painting of Salisbury with the cathedral so dominant may have been of interest to the Hume family to Salisbury given their significant links to the city (John's son Thomas Henry also held office in the diocese).

Next door to the north is the Walton Canonry. William Dodwell, Canon Residentiary and Archdeacon of Berks, lived there from 1754 to 1785. It is possible that some small alterations to the house were made by Canon Dodwell, but his other interests are unknown.

In the painting the most prominent house within the Close is Myles Place, which had lay occupants throughout the 18th century. From 1744 the lease was held by Henry Hele until his death in 1778. Dr Hele was one of the first physicians at Salisbury Infirmary, and if the painting was his he surely would have ensured the new infirmary was included. In his will he left substantial bequests, but unfortunately from the point of view of this investigation, he did not specify individual items, referring only to 'my plate, china, linen, pictures, books ...'.[68]

For much of the 18th century the King's House was leased by members of the Beach family from Keevil Manor and Fittleton who sublet to other tenants,[69] perhaps unlikely candidates for any connection to the painting.

Facing south on The Green, (later called Choristers' Square) there is Mompesson House built by Charles Mompesson in 1701 (see above on whether this is indeed represented). Thomas Hayter and his family lived there for the second half of the 18th century. Hayter is described as 'a prominent citizen' but again, their disposable income and artistic interests are unknown. However, he was sufficiently wealthy to lend money to Bathurst at Clarendon.[70]

Buildings elsewhere in the Close are not visible in the painting but might furnish some further possibilities of interested individuals and families: Along the North Walk No 19, now part of Sarum College, was the Theological College in the nineteenth and twentieth centuries, and before that the home of members of the Hearst and Wyndham families from 1710 to 1797, and Wyndhams again from 1828 to 1860. See St Edmund's College below for more on the Wyndham family.

The Harris family lived at No 15 the Close, later Malmesbury House. James Harris (1709-1780) inherited the house and an independent income on the death of his father in 1733. He had literary, dramatic, political and scientific interests, but his main passion was music. He organised concerts in London and in Salisbury, and was a great supporter and admirer of Handel. Would he have diverted any of his resources into a large painting when there were musical demands on them?

At the Bishop's Palace (now Salisbury Cathedral School) was Bishop John Hume, whose brother lived at Leadenhall. As previously considered, this family was a potential patron for the painting.

Outside the Close there are other suggestions. Alderman William Hussey built The Hall in New St soon after the middle of the 18th century. It is the second largest dwelling house in the city, after The College.[71] William Hussey was Mayor in 1758 and MP for Salisbury from 1774 to 1813. He was a generous benefactor to the city, providing funds for furnishings in the new Council House, street lighting, and other charitable purposes.[72] A painting such as this could have been commissioned to mark the association of the Hussey family with Salisbury over many generations.

St Edmund's College is just visible in the painting to the right of St Edmunds Church. Henry Penruddock Wyndham (1736-1819) was a member of a family that had great influence in Salisbury from the 17th into the 19th centuries. Pen, as he was known, was a freeman of the city, was sheriff of the county in 1772, elected MP for Wiltshire in 1812 and perhaps most significantly, was mayor of Salisbury 1770-1. He had made a 'Grand Tour' for two years from 1765, which he apparently enjoyed but returned unimpressed by what he had seen.[73] Might he have commissioned a painting by an *English* artist of his home town where he was about to hold the main civic office?[74]

Benjamin Collins (1715-1785) was a local entrepreneur, successful provincial bookseller and newspaper proprietor.[75] He had been involved in the trade with his brother William from the 1730s and took control in the following decade, developing the printing, publishing and bookselling enterprise, in particular the production of the *Salisbury Journal*. His residence and business premises were on the New Canal. From 1770 Collins relinquished day to day control but maintained an active management interest in what had become a very profitable firm. He began styling himself 'Gentleman and Banker of Salisbury', and had his portrait painted, but there is no evidence of any other interest in art. He might have desired a dramatic view of the city on which his commercial success was based, even though but he did not take an active part in other institutions or organisations of Salisbury. In his will he left substantial sums and property to his wife and children, but again referred only to 'goods, chattels and personal estate'.[76]

It should be borne in mind that there is no direct evidence at all for any of these people in or around Salisbury being involved with this painting. Some, like the first Earl of Radnor, are perhaps more likely candidates than others but until confirmation is unearthed, the reader may come to their own conclusions. Without any doubt the artist has provided a dramatic view of the city of Salisbury.

An afterword

This article has been written by historians – of architecture and local society. There is more work that could be done of course, by others, which would generate a different interpretation. An art historian looking at the painting might see an Arcadian landscape under a vast radiant sky. The major focal point on the right – Clarendon Park – is emphasised with the double rainbow. Salisbury Cathedral dramatically holds centre stage, and to the left on the horizon is Old Sarum. So are these symbols representing God's relationship with the people via monarch, church and parliament, reinforced with the promise offered by the rainbow? Perhaps these three key places were intended to be linked by the river, on which sails a boat – are the colours of the pennant and clothing significant? There are no doubt many possible suggestions; probably everyone who sees the images will have their own ideas. The contributions received are much appreciated.

The painting will continue to attract interest and to generate debate, discussion and probably controversy, all adding to the excitement of looking at it closely, asking what it might (or might not) tell us about 18th century Salisbury, and thinking about who painted it and who wanted it created.

Acknowledgements

We would like to thank John Crook for his photographs of the painting and for producing the key and map. In the course of looking closely at the painting, and investigating its contents and possible history, we have consulted works of reference which are indicated below, and discussed the project with experts in libraries, archives, sale rooms, galleries and amongst our friends and colleagues. Without their knowledge and encouragement this paper would be the poorer, and we extend to them our grateful thanks. Fred and Kathryn Uhde, who have this painting hanging on the wall in their home, have given us their enthusiastic support.

Notes

1   Sotheby's, Sale Catalogue of British Paintings, 1500-1858 (9 – 16 July, 1986), item no 79

2   *Ibid*

3   *Export of Works of Art, 1986-87* (HMSO 1987), 19-20, Case 15

4   This was still quite a large industry in the mid-18th century – see Chandler, John, 1983, *Endless Street, a history of Salisbury and its people*, Hobnob Press, 73-92. Tentering racks are shown just north of St Edmund's church on William Naish's map of Salisbury (2nd edition, 1751). See note 8 below.

5   Later marked as trig-points on the Ordnance Survey maps at 353 ft (West) and 345 ft above sea-level. The Cathedral Close ground level in Salisbury is, very roughly, 150 ft above sea-level, making the top of the 400ft spire about 550 ft above sea-level. By contrast, the highest point of Old Sarum castle is about 400 ft above sea-level, and the highest ground on the western side of Clarendon Park, ie just above the prominent spire of St Martin's church, Salisbury (see below) is, according to the Ordnance Survey, 486 ft above sea-level (or 477 ft in the later editions. The

heights are best shown on the 1:2500 Ordnance survey maps, surveyed in 1878-9, and revised in 1900. The OS 6 inch sheets, surveyed in 1923-4, have more accurate contours, with some revisions in 1938-57. I am grateful to the Salisbury Reference Librarians for access to these.

6 Just out of the picture is the start of the 'New Canal Navigation', a boat canal, started in 1675, to connect Salisbury with the sea. The course of this canal, and the River Avon, are shown on Naish's map (see below).

7 See Rogers, K H, 1963, 'Naish's Map of Salisbury', first published in 1716, *Wiltshire Archaeological & Natural History Society Magazine (WANHM)* 58, 453-4. The area is first accurately shown in FJ Kelsey's 'Map of the Tithing of East Harnham in the Parish of Britford' (1846).

8 In 1753-4, see VCH *Wiltshire IV* (1959), 259.

9 Pencil sketch, in Private Collection, Reynolds 11.24.

10 Now in the Art Institute, Williamstown, Mass, USA.

11 Engraving on paper in Salisbury and South Wilts Museum.

12 RCHM, 1980, *City of Salisbury*, HMSO, 51. See also Chandler, John, 2013, 'Harnham Bridge' in Howells, Jane (ed) *Harnham Historical Miscellany*, 59-79.

13 Perhaps first built in the 17th century. See RCHM, 1980, 131, monument 331.

14 RCHM, 1980, 54-6.

15 See Hall, P, 1834, *Picturesque Memorials of Salisbury*, plate 17.

16 Now Tollgate Road

17 See RCHM, 1993, *Salisbury, the houses of the Close*, HMSO, 240-3 for a more detailed history.

18 The open meadow immediately to the right (south-east) of the South Canonry is today a sports field, known as Rack Close. No cloth drying racks are shown here in the picture, but Naish's early 18th century map (note 8 above) does show some drying racks here.

19 The 1649 Parliamentary survey of the Close mentions 'the walk planted with young Elmes'. *Trans. Salisbury Field Club*, I (1893), 135.

20 Of 18th century Flemish bond, see RCHM, 1993, 243

21 RCHM, 1993, 243-4

22 These are best shown in Buckler's 1809 watercolour, as they were before the 19th century restoration. See RCHM, 1993, 55 plate 22.

23 It is entitled 'General Plan of the Bishop of Salisbury's Palace' and still hangs in the Palace (now the Cathedral School). See Tatton-Brown, T, (2002), 'A New View of Salisbury', *Country Life*, 196, 186-7

24 The gabled roof to the left may be the palace stables. To the right of this, smoke is seen coming from a chimney.

25 Cocke, T and Kidson, P, 1993, *Salisbury Cathedral: Perspectives on the Architectural History*, 48, plate 48.

26 For fuller details, see Tatton-Brown, T, 1995, 'The Cloisters of Salisbury Cathedral' *Spire* 65, 6-10. See also the Chapter Act Book (below, note 31).

27 See note 15, plate 24, where they are still prominent.

28 RCHM, 1993, 231-240.

29 RCHM, 1993, 226-231

30 These are carefully delineated in Thacker's engraving (note 25, above).

31 Chapter Act Book 21 (1741-1796). I am most grateful to Suzanne Eward for a copy of her transcriptions of these.

32 There were continuing separate orders about the disposal of the bells, and finally in 1790, the whole of the rest of the bell-tower was demolished.

33 RCHM, 1993, 189 and 201.

34 RCHM, 1980, 36-9, after the earlier central tower had collapsed in 1653.

35 RCHM, 1980, 48. See also Wilcockson, Helen, 2007, 'College to Council House' *Sarum Chronicle* 7, illustrations p 19 and 23.

36 It actually sits on a small truncated spire. RCHM, 1980, 29

37 RCHM, 1980, 76.

38 Naish, and the First edition OS (1:500) map show 'The Green' best. The former has fences (?) on the south and trees on the western edges.

39 RCHM, 1980, 52-3

40 Salisbury Guildhall collection. www.bbc.co.uk/arts/yourpaintings.

41 This church was sadly demolished in 1852, though some of the masonry of the tower was recycled in the new tower of St Paul's church, built further north in the same year. RCHM, 1980, 41. See also Wright, Trevor, 2007, 'The last days of St Clements church', *Sarum Chronicle* 7, 2-12.

42 Demolished in 1970 and 1972 respectively. The mid-18th century Fisherton Mill House still stands. RCHM, 1980, 159.

43 RCHM, 1980, 176-8.

44 See, for example, McNeill, J, 2005, *Old Sarum*, English Heritage Guide, 37-8. The Tree, an elm, was apparently finally cut down in 1905.

45 For finer depictions of Old Sarum from the south, by John Constable in 1829, see Wilcox, T, 2011, *Constable and Salisbury*, 168-173.

46 These buildings, which are the closest to the artist in the whole picture, are partly covered up, and the wet paint seems to have been smudged by the original frame. For details of this 16th century building, with 17th and 18th century enlargements, see RCHM, 1980, 170. See also a modern photograph in Howells, Jane (ed), 2013, 118.

47 Reproduced in Howells, Jane (ed), 2013, 130.

48 For details of his life and work see ODNB

49 It is now in the Hepworth collection at Wakefield, and is said to have been painted in 1800

50 There are two swans and a group of figures in a rowing boat in another Richards painting, bearing some similarity with the birds in the middle foreground of our picture.

51 Tate Online. Richards, belltower, Salisbury ref T093342

52 ODNB

53 Email correspondence Uhde with Carlton-Jones Dec 2013

54 VCH Wiltshire Vol 6 p 92. Durman R, 2007, *Milford*, Sarum Studies, 26

55 www.duffhouse.org.uk/history/

56 Montcoffer House listing, Historic Scotland building ID 6649.

57 In 1900 by special remainder the dukedom could pass to daughters and their male issue, so following his death his elder daughter Princess Alexandra succeeded as Duchess of Fife. Obituary of the Princes Royal, *The Times*, 5 January 1931 p 17

58 *The Times* Feb 10 1932 p 9

59 Catalogues of sales at Christies, I would like to thank the Librarian Lynda McLeod for her assistance.

60 Lees-Milne, James, 1986, *Earls of Creation,* National Trust, 1986 title page

61 The Folly is, however, not apparently shown on Andrews and Dury's fine map of Wiltshire (1773) and is only first accurately shown on Kelsey's 1846 map (note 8, above). A clump of trees here (near the 'One Mile Tree' on the road, one mile from Harnham Bridge) is shown on the 'Plan of the Encampments near Salisbury' map of 1778 and 1779, British Library, Add.MS15533-131r. See Chandler, John, 2008, 'Two neglected early maps', *Sarum Chronicle* 8, 37

62 WSA MR Box 47 1946/3/2A/1

63 Beaumont James, Tom and Gerrard, Christopher, 2007, *Clarendon Landscape of Kings,* Windgather Press Macclesfield, 109

64 Will of Peter Bathurst proved 26 January 1802 TNA PROB 11/1368/276, focuses on the estate and timber, with a reference to 'the household furniture, pictures, libraries of books in my dwelling house at Clarendon Park'.

65 VCH 6, ODNB, Richards, David, 2012, 'Old Sarum, the Pitts and their Diamond', *Sarum Chronicle* 12

66 www.shaftesburyestates.com/stgileshouse.php

67 Information on these houses and their occupants, especially South Canonry and Leadenhall from note supplied by John Bushell, to whom we extend our grateful thanks for his initial work on this subject. Also RCHME, 1993. Ross, Christopher, 2000, *The Canons of Salisbury*, Dean & Chapter.

68 Will of Henry Hele proved 9 July 1778 TNA PROB11/1044/50

69 Newman, Ruth, 2010, *Living in the King's House*, and 2012, *The Buildings of the King's House*, Salisbury & South Wiltshire Museum information pamphlets. Beach family archive at Gloucester Archives has no relevant reference (with thanks to John Chandler).

70 James and Gerrard, 109

71 RCHME, 1980, 105b

72 www.salisburycitycouncil.gov.uk

73 ODNB Henry Penruddock Wyndham. Wilcockson, Helen, 2007, 'College to Council House', *Sarum Chronicle* 7, 2007 19-30

74 Will of HP Wyndham proved 23 June 1819 TNA PROB 11/1617/353, largely concerns succession of estates; I cannot see any bequests of individual possessions except reference to 'my goods and chattels', but it is *very* difficult handwriting, and copy.

75 Ferdinand, C Y, 1997, *Benjamin Collins and the provincial newspaper trade in the eighteenth century*, OUP. Thanks to Ruth Newman for suggesting Collins as a possible candidate.

76 *ibid* Appendix: Wills, the will of Benjamin Collins

Out of the shadows: who was Chevalier J O C Grant of Sarum?

David Algar and Peter Saunders

When the signature on an interesting painting is unfamiliar there is a natural inclination to want to know more about the artist so when we saw the name 'Chev^r. J. Grant' on a small watercolour, recently acquired by Salisbury Museum,[1] we were curious to discover who he was. He proved to be a character completely invisible to standard reference books and histories and thus we embarked upon the task of bringing him out of the

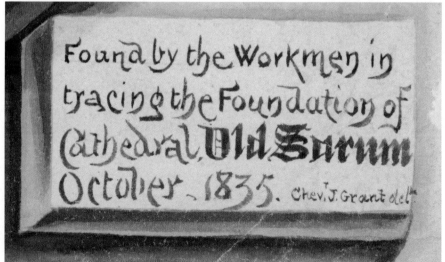

The title and signature placed by Jasper Grant on his watercolour of archaeological remains from the 1835 excavations at Old Sarum. We may only speculate whether he painted them when he viewed them in an exhibition or whether he was commissioned to do so by the excavators. The 'label', as also the map in his portrait of a lady, provided an ideal vehicle for the artist's name.

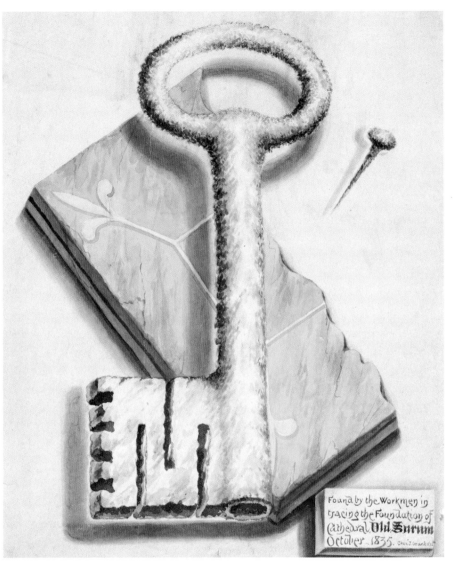

The watercolour which began the search for Jasper Grant's story: 'Found by the Workmen in tracing the Foundation of Cathedral. Old Sarum. October 1835' by 'Chevr. J. Grant'. Courtesy of Salisbury Museum (SBYWM: 2011.12).

shadows. The fruits of our research will hopefully prove sufficient to allow Grant a modest place in the history of Salisbury people as well as proving him now worthy of at least a footnote in the record of minor Victorian artists. A list of works by Grant located by us appears as an appendix but this is likely to be far from complete: having brought him to attention, we hope this will encourage the identification of more of his work.

The watercolour seen in Salisbury Museum depicts a large iron key, a tile fragment and a pin or nail, with, in the bottom right hand corner, what appears to be a block bearing a display label upon which is written: 'Found by the Workmen in tracing the Foundation of Cathedral. Old Sarum October 1835. Chev[r]. J. Grant del[t].'. Of the objects portrayed, only the key is known today so this work has some value as an archaeological record. The tile fragment is probably medieval[2] though Grant's depiction appears to be simplified and is not very convincing, being shown as if 'laminated'. Inlaid floor tiles from Old Sarum are uncommon. There is now no record of the small pin or nail, its apparent lack of corrosion suggesting that it may have been a decorative stud of copper alloy. The paper used for the painting bears the watermark of the Kentish paper-maker Ruse and Turner and the date 1834.

By a remarkable coincidence this painting was acquired by the Museum just as we were preparing for publication a catalogue of its collection of medieval keys. The key,[3] the principal subject illustrated, had been found in 1835 during excavations by Henry Hatcher following a notably dry summer which had caused the cathedral foundations at Old Sarum to appear as parch marks of unusual clarity. It was described as being recovered 'near to the site of the west door'.[4] From the size of the key and its find-spot, it is tempting to suggest that it was the key to the great west door of the 12th century

'The College', pen and wash, 1831. Courtesy of Salisbury Museum (SBYWM: 1902-03.1.4.1).

Chevr. Grant's signature on 'The College'.

cathedral. Grant's depiction of the key is pleasingly faithful to the original.

Chevalier J Grant clearly had access to these recently discovered finds from Old Sarum, which suggested to us that he might be local man. Who was he? What other works of his could be located? When did he flourish? Enquiries of national sources revealed nothing of his work but, locally, answers did begin to emerge. In Salisbury Museum there is a print of Salisbury Cathedral, dated 1845, and a sepia pen and wash drawing entitled 'The College', signed 'Chev[r]. Grant. Del[t]: 1831'. St Edmund's Church is included in the picture, to the left of the College (now called the Council House), the whole executed from a vantage point at the north end of Greencroft Street. The Wiltshire Museum, Devizes has a lithograph, 'Wilton Church', with the signature 'Chev. J O C Grant, del Sarum 1846'.[5] These are competent works, the latter in particular incorporating people, vegetation and sky to create an attractive picture.

The subject matter and dates of these works suggested that Chevalier J O C Grant may have worked in Salisbury in the 1830s and 1840s. Public records were to prove this so and have allowed us to locate his place of birth, marriage and death. He was born on 17th October 1804, the son of John and Elizabeth Grant of 26 St Martin's le Grand, Westminster, Middlesex. He was baptised Jasper Octavius Grant in November 1804 at Christ Church and St Leonard, Foster Lane.[6] It is not known why but by 1831 he is styling himself 'Chevalier'.[7] Perhaps this was an affectation to boost his sense of self-importance? By 1833 he had also added 'C' as a third initial to his name (for César).[8] On 27th April 1843 he married Sarah, daughter of Thomas Nicholas, a painter, of Fisherton Anger, at St Martin's Church, Salisbury.[9] They had one child, a daughter, Eliza Algerina Harriet, baptised on 28th August 1848.[10]

From the time of his birth until the unknown date of his arrival in Salisbury his life remains an enigma. However, his father is known to have been a woollen draper, which hints towards the background in which Grant would have spent his early years.[11] He appears in the Salisbury census returns for 1841 and 1851 - and in that of Southampton for 1861. In 1841 Jasper Grant is noted as living at Caves Buildings, Exeter Street, Salisbury.[12] This tenement block is called Queens Terrace on the 'Salisbury Local Board of Health: Plan of District' of 1854.[13] It later became Exeter Terrace and was demolished during the redevelopment of the Friary area in the late 1960s. He is described as an artist and it is of interest to note that Sarah is recorded with his surname, although they did not marry until 1843. The St Martin Rate Books show that they left Exeter Street early in 1849. By 1851 the census records Jasper O C Grant living in Salt Lane, Salisbury with his wife and daughter. The anti-clockwise route taken by the census recorder from Greencroft Street indicates that his cottage was the second in Salt Lane, later numbered 46 and also subsequently demolished.[14] Now he is described as a 'drawing master and carver'.[15]

Beyond his employment nothing is known of Grant's rôle within local society, apart from his membership of the Ancient Order of Foresters. In July 1846 'Brother J O C Grant, P C R' [Past Chief Ranger] was presented with a silver medal by the brethren of Court 'Robin Hood' for his praiseworthy

'Wilton Church', print, 1846. © Wiltshire Museum, Devizes (DZSWS: 1983.2326).

conduct as a past officer. A contemporary report of this event, held during a Court night at the Goat Inn, Milford Street, notes that in a 'neat and appropriate address' he thanked 'the fraternity for the distinguished honour they had bestowed'.[16]

His use of the term 'Chevalier' – in its literal sense, a man of honour – may indicate a wish to present himself as more important than he was to boost his image, hoping perhaps to further his standing within the community or to attract patronage. If so, he doubtless took pride in the commercially-attractive wording: 'Dedicated by the express permission of

Portrait of a lady, watercolour, 1833. Private ownership.

Sarum Chronicle 14 page 43

We regret, and take responsibility for, the omission of a significant quotation following the colon in the centre of this page. It should read as follows:

Your rather masculine looking lady: I think that she is spot on for the 1833 date and I have to say that Chev J O C Grant was rather a good observer of dress. True she seems to have lost her left forearm, but the details of the dress from the way that the pleats fall on the bodice of the dress to the curls in the hairstyle are nicely observed.

The sitter wears what is likely to be an evening dress (both because of the low wide style of the neckline and because of the sheen effect of the dress which suggests that the fabric is a silk, a plain darker-coloured silk). The bodice of the dress is pleated either side of the centre front, with the pleats running down diagonally to converge at a point at the centre front of what appears to be a separate belt with a central buckle, all of which emphasize a slender waist. The skirt of the dress (the bodice and skirt would have been all-in-one at this date) looks like it was pleated on to the waistband, probably with a technique called cartridge pleating (which looks just like a row of cartridges) at this date.

The major feature of the dress is the huge gigot sleeves, which were likely to be padded to give that enormous puffed effect.

In terms of jewellery, she is wearing a long double string of small coloured beads, which is looped at the waist, a popular fashion at this date. The brooch too, worn at the central point of the bodice, was fashionable. I'm surprised she isn't wearing dangling ear-rings, and that velvet choker seems a little unusual for this date. I've been looking at a couple of illustrations, and generally the neck is bare, almost as if an uncluttered swan-like neck was the look to go for.

Her hairstyle is great. She has sausage-shaped side curls and a top-knot, which was known as an Apollo knot, with a tortoiseshell comb behind.

Her Most Gracious Majesty Queen Victoria',[17] which was used to publicise a lithograph derived from his drawing of an 'extraordinary bird', a bird he had in 1840 'forwarded to Buckingham Palace by the express desire and command of her Majesty'.[18]

By 1861 Jasper Grant and his family had left Salisbury to live in Southampton, where they are found sharing a house at 12 Edward Street, St Mary's with Charles Coe, a dock labourer, his wife and four children. Grant's profession is now described as 'land surveyor',[19] any pretence to his being an artist apparently abandoned. Coe was born in Salisbury so there may already have been some connection with the Grant family. Jasper died in January 1864, aged 59.[20] His wife, Sarah, outlived him and was recorded in 1871 living at 91 High Street, Southampton, employed as a general domestic servant.[21]

By a lucky coincidence, as we embarked on this research, 'Wigs on the Green Fine Art', York was offering for sale a half-length watercolour portrait, in a contemporary ebonised frame, of a lady in a green dress.[22] This lady, as yet unidentified, is painted seated by a table upon which a map has been spread out. The map appears to show an unfinished outline of Wiltshire and Somerset, in a panel at the top of which the artist has written his name 'Chevalier J. O. C. Grant Del^t. 1833'. The lady holds a sealed letter which she appears to have just written; her quill pen and bottle of ink stand on the table. Rosemary Harden of the Fashion Museum, Bath comments on this portrait:

This is the only portrait by Jasper Grant as yet located and thus perhaps we should not be surprised that he is absent from directories of Victorian painters and is unknown to the National Portrait Gallery. It is, however, interesting that Grant uses an unfinished map as the vehicle to carry his signature in this portrait, for later, in the 1861 census, he is described as a land surveyor. Previously he seems to have regarded himself as an artist or drawing master but all these activities would depend on his skill as a draughtsman, for which he certainly had a good eye. The only other indication of his work in this field is a watercolour: 'Plan of the Belmont Estate situate in the parish of Laverstock...from an actual Survey taken AD 1835 by J.O.C.Grant, Sarum.'[23]

The bulk of Grant's oeuvre focuses on topographical illustrations of landscapes and buildings. These divide into original drawings and watercolours, and others known only from engravings in print form, some illustrating books. Grant seems to have had some success in preparing work to be engraved as vignettes, illustrations that shade away at the edges, which enjoyed great popularity at the time.

Apart from the views of Salisbury Cathedral, the College and Wilton

THE HALLE OF JOHN HALLE.

Church mentioned above, there also exist an engraving of Wilton House[24] and, published as illustrations in (J. B., 1848), views of the Poultry Cross and the interior of the Halle of John Halle in Salisbury, with another of Wilton Church in the 1856 edition. It was also Grant's intention in 1847 to 'publish a view of Norman Court [Winterslow], the seat of C. B. Wall, Esq., M.P., one of the highly-respected Members for this city'.[25]

Farther afield, in Hampshire, he prepared two views: 'Town Hall and buildings in the Market Place, Basingstoke', dated 1831, and 'Holy Ghost Chapel, Basingstoke', undated but likely to be of similar date. Grant apparently travelled to Dorset in 1833–4, when 13 illustrations of the Weymouth area were produced.[26]

There are two works of subject matter very different from all the others recorded here. The first, from 1840, is an illustration of 'an extraordinary BIRD, at present unknown and undescribed by Naturalists, which was recently caught at Fresh Water Cave, Isle of Wight'.[27] This was offered for sale by subscription as 'A SPLENDID LITHOGRAPHED DRAWING', India proofs priced at 10s, plain at 5s. The second is a drawing '… of an animal half deer and half horse', a creature 'of great curiosity' owned by

'The Poultry Cross', used to illustrate The Salisbury Guide, 1848. It lacks finesse, perhaps drawn in haste to meet a deadline or reflecting a decline in Grant's skill at this time.

Mr Attwater of Bodenham. This work of 1848 was described as 'a beautiful drawing … from the pencil of Mr J O C Grant of this city'.[28] In recording unfamiliar creatures did Grant possess a particular talent or did he have an eye for a commercial opportunity?

In the early 19th century transparencies were a popular art form using colour and light to enhance festivities and other notable events.[29] The artistic draughtsmanship of a man like Grant might be expected to have been much in demand and in 1839 we know he produced some for the celebration of Edmund Antrobus's 21st birthday: 'At the entrance of Aversham [sic: Amesbury] park, the family crest was illuminated, and which had a pretty effect. Several transparencies, executed by Chevalier Grant, were exhibited. One of these were [sic] in front of Mr Bettie's house, (surgeon). The design was emblematical of the event, and bearing Antrobus's coat of arms and in the centre of which were the Figures "21" and underneath the following Latin inscription -"Vive Valeque", and another at Mr Casse's, representing the horn of plenty, and "E.A. may you be blessed with health and happiness".' Among the decorations in the ballroom there was 'a transparency of her most gracious Majesty Queen Victoria', which is also likely to have been created by Grant.[30]

The art work so far discovered is all dated within the two decades of the 1830s and 40s. For much of this period Grant was living in Exeter Street. It is noted that after the birth of his daughter and subsequent move to Salt Lane his sources of income seem to move away from artistic endeavour. His known artistic works come to a rather abrupt end in 1849. We do not know the reason for this but it is conceivable that he may have been affected adversely in some way by the epidemics which had such a devastating effect on life in Salisbury at this time.[31] In 1851, however, he is calling himself a drawing master so he was possibly employed teaching the art of drawing in school[32] or even from home. He did not contribute to the 1852 Salisbury Exhibition held in the Guildhall,[33] where the displays were to be recorded in two lithographs by his fellow artist, Walter Tiffin. Apart from Tiffin, however, Grant was still the only other artist listed in Salisbury in a directory of 1855.[34]

In the 1851 census Grant's occupation is also given as 'carver'. No evidence of his work in this respect has come to our attention but a newspaper report in 1847 records that he 'forwarded to Lord Arundell, at Wardour Castle, a beautiful model, carved in stone, of the Roman Catholic Church of St Osmund, now in course of erection in Salisbury, with which his Lordship expressed himself much pleased'.[35] Efforts to locate this model have thus far proved fruitless. The foundation stone of the church had been laid on 8th April 1847 and the building was consecrated in September 1848. At this time, Grant was still living very close by in Exeter Street.

Jasper Grant was working as the local agent for the Commercial and General Life Assurance Association in 1847.[36] In the Post Office Directory of 1855, he is listed as an artist and insurance agent, but now living in Salt Lane.[37] Another advertisement, in 1857, gives more specific information about this employment: he is one of the two local agents acting for the Norfolk Farmers' Cattle Insurance Society.[38]

More has been discovered about Jasper Grant than we thought possible when we first viewed his picture of objects from Old Sarum but our research has not been exhaustive: what remains to be told of his story is for others to explore. Sadly for an artist, we have no likeness of him. His early life remains uncharted. The impression we have of him is that he was never really as successful an artist as perhaps he had hoped to be. He was not without talent and was more than someone who painted or drew simply for pleasure. Yet his primary employment as an artist seemingly failed him in later life.[39] He did, however, have other sources of income: as a land surveyor, as a cartographer and as a carver, about which we can only surmise as little solid evidence has thus far emerged. In the end he had to make his way in the commercial world, trading his talent and picking up commissions wherever he could: if not as an artist, then as an insurance agent, teacher or land agent – impoverished artists, like actors, have always struggled!

Finally, near the end of his life we find him living in a less than salubrious area of Southampton sharing a house with a dock labourer and his family

Transcript of an advertisement in the *Salisbury and Winchester Journal*, 16 May, 1857, one of several providing evidence of Grant's employment as an insurance agent.

NORFOLK FARMERS' CATTLE INSURANCE SOCIETY.
Established 1849.
CHIEF OFFICES – ST. GILES STREET, NORWICH.

For insuring the Owners of all kinds of Live Stock against
Loss in case of Death from Disease or Accident.
Rates reduced to the lowest point consistent with security.
Prospectus containing full information may be obtained
on application to
CHARLES R. GILMAN, Secretary,
or any of the Local Agents or Inspectors.
AGENTS AT SALISBURY:
Mr. WYNDHAM PAIN, Castle Brewery.
Mr. J. O. C. GRANT, Salt Lane.
AGENTS WANTED.

– far removed from the high-class patronage he had enjoyed earlier in his career. But Jasper's life was not without historical interest and it seems fitting that on the 150th anniversary of his death he should emerge from obscurity for a brief moment in the limelight.[40]

Appendix: List of known art work

1831 'The College', signed 'Chev^r. Grant. Del^t :1831'. Pen and wash. Salisbury Museum.

1831 'View of the Town Hall and buildings in the Market Place, Basingstoke as they appeared in the year 1831; Chevalier J O Grant pinxit; R Martin lithog. 124 High Holborn'. Lithograph. Hampshire County Museum Service.

Undated 'Holy Ghost Chapel, Basingstoke; Chevalier J O C Grant pinxt; Printed by C Hullmandel'. Lithograph. Hampshire County Museum Service.

1833 Portrait of a lady in a green dress, signed 'Chevalier J. O. C. Grant Del^t 1833'. Watercolour. Private collection, Halifax, Nova Scotia, Canada.

1833 'Sandsfoot Castle and Portland; Chevalier Grant del^t. 1833; R Martin Lith, 124 H Holborn; Published by B Bensen, Weymouth'. Lithograph National Trust Collection, Kingston Lacy.

In the Bussell Collection, Weymouth Museum, 12 original sketches:

1833 'Ferry House, near Weymouth', pencil and wash; 'Lulworth Chapel', pencil and wash; 'Lulworth Castle', pen and wash; 'Southdown Cottage, near Weymouth', pencil; 'Fleet Church, near Weymouth', pen and wash; 'Pennsylvania Castle and Ruins of church: Rufus Castle, Portland', pen and wash; 'Pennsylvania Castle,

Portland', pen and wash; 'Portland Church, (St George)', pen and wash; 'Burning Cliff, near Weymouth,' pencil and wash; 'Radipole Spa, near Weymouth', pencil and wash; and 1834 'Burning Cliff, near Weymouth', pen and wash; 'Radipole, near Weymouth', pencil and wash.

1835 'Found by the Workmen in tracing the Foundation of Cathedral. Old Sarum October 1835. Chev[r] J Grant del[t]'. Watercolour. Salisbury Museum.

1835 'Plan of the Belmont Estate situate in the parish of Laverstock...from an actual Survey taken AD 1835 by J.O.C.Grant, Sarum.' Watercolour. Unlocated.

1839 Two transparencies prepared for the 21st birthday celebrations of Edmund Antrobus of Amesbury Park, Wiltshire: Antrobus's coat of arms, figure 21 superimposed and motto 'Vive Valeque'; Horn of Plenty with salutary text. Possibly another, of Queen Victoria. Unlikely to be extant.

1840 Illustration of an extraordinary bird from Freshwater Cave, Isle of Wight. Lithograph. Unlocated.

1845 'Salisbury Cathedral; Chev[r]. J. O. C. Grant del[t] Sarum, 1845; Madley, lith. 3, Wellington S[t] Strand'. Lithograph. Salisbury Museum.

1846 'Wilton Church; Chev[r] J. O. C. Grant del Sarum 1846; Madley, litho 3 Wellington S[t] Strand'. Lithograph. Wiltshire Museum, Devizes.

In *The Salisbury Guide* by J. B. (1848) are illustrations entitled 'The Halle of John Halle' (Chev[r] Grant) and 'Poultry Cross' (Chev[r] Grant). The edition of 1856 also includes 'Wilton Church' (Chev[r] J.O.C. Grant).

1847 Model in stone of St Osmund's Church, Salisbury. Unlocated.

1847 View of Norman Court, intention to publish recorded.

1848 Drawing of an extraordinary animal owned by Mr Attwater of Bodenham. Unlocated.

1849 'Wilton House; Chev[r], J.O.C. Grant, del[t].; Rock & C[o]. London Oct[r] 20th 1849. N[o] 1228.' Steel vignette.

Undated 'Wilton Church, Wilts; Pub[d]. F. A. Blake. Salisbury; Printed by A. La Riviere, 18 Clifton St, Finsbury; Grant Del[t].' Lithograph. Wiltshire Museum, Devizes (DZSWS:1983.1858).

Acknowledgements

We are particularly grateful to Tony and Elizabeth Light for advice and considerable help in locating sources referring to Grant; David Cousins for his photographic expertise; Steven Hobbs and Michael Marshman (Wiltshire and Swindon History Centre, Chippenham) for help with archives; Rosemary Harden (Fashion Museum, Bath) for her description of the costume depicted in the portrait of a lady in a green dress; and Dr Roger Logan (Foresters' Heritage Trust) for information about the Court 'Robin Hood'.

The following are thanked for their help and advice, readily given: Gill Arnott (Hampshire County Museum Service), Dr R P Attrill (bird recorder for the Isle of Wight), Arthur Bowden, Colin Brain, Paul Cox (National

Portrait Gallery), Michael Foulis, Norman Hall, Alison Harding, (Natural History Museum, London), Jane Howells, Barrie Kempthorne, Ruth Newman, Peter O'Donoghue (York Herald, College of Arms), Heather Ault, Lisa Brown and Susan Roderick (Wiltshire Museum, Devizes), and Rhian Wong (Royal Collection Trust).

We acknowledge with gratitude the permission of Salisbury Museum and the Wiltshire Museum, Devizes to reproduce images of work in their care. We hope that this article may bring to light further work by Grant to grow Salisbury Museum's collection of work by this hitherto unrecognised Salisbury artist.

Bibliography

Anon, 1864, *Descriptive Catalogue of the Salisbury & South Wilts Museum,* Salisbury Museum

Knecht, R J, 1962, 'Schools' in E Crittall (ed) *Victoria County History of Wiltshire,* 6, 161-8

Eames, E, 1991, 'Tiles' in P and E Saunders (eds) *Salisbury Museum Medieval Catalogue Part 1,* Salisbury Museum

Benson, R and Hatcher, H, 1843, *Old and New Sarum or Salisbury,* Nichols and Son

Howells, J and Newman, R, 2011 (eds) *William Small's Cherished Memories and Associations,* Wiltshire Record Society, 64

J B [John Burchell Moore], 1848, *The Salisbury Guide; or, An Account, Historical and Descriptive, of The Objects of Interest in Salisbury and its Neighbourhood,* Brodie and Co

Newman, R, 2012, 'Salisbury: The struggle for Reform. The 180th anniversary of the great Reform Act, 1832', *Sarum Chronicle* 12, 41-54

Saunders, P, 2009, *Channels to the Past: the Salisbury Drainage Collection,* Salisbury Museum

Schuster, J, Saunders, P and Algar, D, 2012, 'Objects of Iron' in P Saunders (ed) *Salisbury Museum Medieval Catalogue Part 4,* Salisbury Museum

Abbreviations

SJ = *The Salisbury and Winchester Journal*
HJ = *Hampshire Advertiser*
WSA = Wiltshire and Swindon Archives

Notes

1   Salisbury Museum: SBYWM: 2011.12. It measures 17.5cm by 22cm
2   It compares well with design 127 in Eames 1991 fig 37

3   Salisbury Museum: SBYWM: 2000R.5. See Schuster et al. 2012, 162, no.156

4   Benson and Hatcher 1843, 23-4. The key was presented to Salisbury Museum as part of its foundation collection by Mrs Fowler; see Anon, 1864, 62

5   Salisbury Museum SBYWM: 1993.36 and 1902-03.1.4.1; Wiltshire Museum, Devizes: DZSWS: 1983.2326

6   London Metropolitan Archives, Christchurch Newgate Street, Bishops' transcripts of baptisms, marriages and burials, 1804, DL/A/E/057/MS10115, Item 001

7   His name is not listed in the database of members of the Legion of Honour held at the Musée de la Légion d'honneur, Paris. York Herald, College of Arms (pers. comm.) comments: 'this term was so widely used by foreign bodies and organizations that it is not really possible to shed light on its appearance in this case, without more information. It could be taken to imply membership of a foreign body such as an artistic society, an order of knighthood, or similar'

8   César is spelt out in a report in 16 July 1840, p3 col B (Archives départementales de Seine-Maritime)

9   WSA 1899/20

10 WSA 1899/7

11 Post Office Annual Directory (London) for 1808, 119

12 1841 census HO107/1190 bk4 f13 p18. Grant lived only a few doors from William Small, a man probably of not dissimilar social standing. The latter's two-volume memoirs reveal the lives led by ordinary people in early Victorian Salisbury and provide rare contemporary glimpses into the environment in which Grant strived to make a living. See Howells and Newman 2011

13   WSA G23/701/1PC

14 Grant's cottage was one of three adjoining a substantial house, the freehold of all of which was advertised to be auctioned in July that year in *SJ*, 5 May 1851, p2 col B

15 1851 census HO107/1847 f164 p14

16 *SJ*, 11 July 1846, p4 col C; and the following week he is described as Secretary. The records of the Forest Heritage Trust show that Court 'Robin Hood', no 1917 was founded in mid-1845 but was short lived: it is not listed in the Foresters' Directory of Courts beyond 1848. It met fortnightly at the Goat Inn. Grant may have been its first Chief Ranger because Chief Rangers (chairmen) normally held office for six or 12 months

17 *HJ*, 11 July 1840, p3 col C

18 *HJ*, 6 June 1840, p2 col G

19 1861 census RG9/675 f88 p20. His name does not appear in Sarah Bendall (ed.), *Dictionary of Land Surveyors and Local Map-Makers of Great Britain and Ireland, 1530-1850* (2nd ed., British Library, 1997)

20 Death Index for Southampton, January – March 1864, vol2c, p23

21 1871 census RG11/1193 f124 p12. By 1891 she is 'living on her own means' with her married daughter, Harriet Warwick, a tailoress at 23 Brunswick Square, St Mary's (1891 census RG12/920 f104 p10)

22 Sold for £295 to Thomas Stone, Halifax, Nova Scotia, Canada

23 Woolley & Wallis, Salisbury: Sale, Aug 24 1999, lot 133

24   Reproduced in 1849 by Rock & Co, a prolific publisher of steel engraved vignette views

25 *SJ,* 18 Dec 1847, p4 col C

26 Bussell Collection, Weymouth Museum, contains 12 and the National Trust Collection one at Kingston Lacy

27 An advertisement in 11 July 1840, p3 col C

28 *Wiltshire Independent,* 2 Nov 1848, p4 col E

29 Transparencies were pictures or inscriptions painted on transparent material, usually paper, varnished and brought to life by light shone from behind, often from a candle flame or oil lamp. See Newman 2012, 49 for a description of their use in Salisbury's celebration of the Reform Act, 1832. Grant may have seen these and conceivably been involved in their creation

30 *HJ,* 7 Sept 1839, p4 col C. The celebrations which lasted over three days included an early use of portable gas lighting set up by Mr Edgington of Salisbury

31 For background see Saunders 2009, 5-7

32 For the range of schools in Salisbury see Knecht, 1962

33 His name does not appear in *Catalogue of the Salisbury Exhibition of local industry, amateur productions, works of art, antiquities, objects of taste, articles of vertu, etc: opened on the twelfth of October, 1852* (3rd edition, Salisbury 1852)

34 *Post Office Directory of Wiltshire,* 1855, p151

35 *SJ,* 18 Dec 1847, p4 col C

36 An advertisement in *SJ,* 26 June 1847, p1 col D

37 *Post Office Directory of Wiltshire,* 1855, p100

38 An advertisement in *SJ,* 16 May 1857, p2 col E

39 The new medium of photography was yet to enjoy its explosion in popularity and cannot entirely account for his apparent failure to prosper as an artist

40 The watercolour, which inspired this research, is now on display in Salisbury Museum's Wessex Gallery.

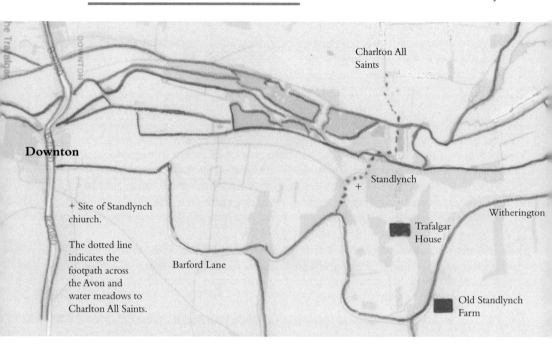

Charlton All
Saints

Downton

Standlynch
+

Witherington

+ Site of Standlynch
chiurch.

Trafalgar
House

The dotted line
indicates the
footpath across
the Avon and
water meadows to
Charlton All Saints.

Barford Lane

Old Standlynch
Farm

Above: Map of the Standlynch area
Below: Trafalgar Park. The central portion was built in 1733. Side wings were added in 1766. It became the home of the Nelson family in 1813 and they remained there until 1947.

Standlynch

John Elliott

Standlynch is located on the eastern bank of the river Avon, about 5 miles south of Salisbury and 2 miles north of Downton. Historically it has always been connected with Charlton All Saints, which is on the western bank of the river, by a footpath and bridge.

Almost certainly there was already a settlement at Standlynch as early as 1016–35; the land having been granted by the Bishop of Winchester and separated from his landholdings in Downton. The settlement is first mentioned in 1086 by which time it had been subdivided into three small estates,[1] though by the sixteenth century the estates had been consolidated into one.

The initial settlement was located above the river crossing and connected by footpath to Witherington, Barford and Downton, and across the river with Charlton All Saints. It was never a wealthy place, and in 1377 there were only 18 poll-tax payers.[2] The population declined in the fifteenth century, though in the sixteenth and seventeenth centuries there was a substantial manor house, church, farmstead, weir and mill.

In 1733 a new, and very substantial, manor house was erected somewhat to the east of the old settlement and this subsequently became Trafalgar House in 1815. A new farm complex (known now as Old Standlynch Farm) was created further east at much the same time along with another farm which was built much closer to the river (Old Dairy Farm).

The nineteenth century witnessed something of an economic revival, almost certainly because of Trafalgar House. The population of 41 in 1801 rose to 107 by 1871 before falling to 72 in 1891 and 67 in 1931. The current population is about 30.

Standlynch has always stood separate from Downton, though for much of its history it has been closely linked with its much bigger neighbour. Between 1897 and 1934 it was joined with Charlton All Saints,[3] but was subsequently reunited within Downton Parish. As we shall see, the occupants of Standlynch often exploited this geographical separation to allow themselves certain religious liberties.

The river crossing at Standlynch which links Standlynch on the east bank of the river Avon with Charlton All Saints on the west (photographs John Elliott)

The manor house that existed in the early eighteenth century was most probably medieval with extensions that dated from the late sixteenth century. It was located on the north side of the current roadway down to the weir and footbridge across the Avon. The house ranged over three sides of a courtyard, the north side being open and giving access to a park. The whole was ruinous by 1748.[4]

In 1733 a new Standlynch House was built somewhat to the east on higher ground with commanding views to the west. The client was Sir Peter Vandeput and the architect Roger Morris (1695-1749). Morris most probably started as a foreman bricklayer and then in 1724 began working as a builder. He was much involved with the eighteenth century development of London and closely linked with Colen Campbell and Henry Herbert, Earl of Pembroke, for whom he worked in London. He also worked for Lord Radnor.

Standlynch House was a somewhat conventional Palladian arrangement with the substantial rooms in the centre and smaller rooms on the four corners. There was a seven bay front and it was built of brick with stone dressings. Substantial 9 bay by 3 bay side wings were added to the north and south in 1766,[5] when the owner was Henry Dawkins, a leading member of the Society of Dilletanti. The Society of Dilletanti was initially established as a London dining club in 1734 by a group of people who had been on the Grand Tour. In 1743 Horace Walpole described it as '...a club, for which the nominal qualification is having been in Italy, and the real one, being drunk'. It claimed that it sponsored the study of ancient Greek and Roman art, and the creation of new work in that style.

John Wood junior was the architect and the internal decoration was handled by Nicolas Revett. John Wood Junior (1728-81) was the son of John Wood (1704-54) of Bath. Both father and son were noted architects and responsible for many buildings in Bath and elsewhere. The son designed the Royal Crescent (1767-75).

Nicholas Revett (1720-1804) was an active member of the Society of Dilletanti and travelled extensively in Greece and Italy, publishing the results. He also designed the Doric porch and Giovanni Battista Cipriani (1727-85) was employed to decorate the room on the south eastern corner of the main house. The most impressive rooms are the cube hall and the staircase.[6]

In the eighteenth century such substantial houses required extensive surrounding parklands which displayed an idealized form of nature and provided an alternative to the formal gardens which had existed previously. So an area of land was emparked at the same time as the house was being built and gardens were created by Charles Bridgeman (1690-1738) who was a leading landscape gardener. His work has since largely been eclipsed by that of his successors William Kent and Lancelot 'Capability' Brown.

Palladianism was an architectural style that dominated the first half of the eighteenth century and was based on the work of the Italian designer Andrea Palladio (1508-80) who was active in Venice and had been influenced by the works of the Roman Vitruvius (c.80-70BC – c.15BC). During the eighteenth century the works of ancient Greece and Rome were seen as the stylistic models which should be copied and evidence of good taste. Most young men of means undertook the Grand Tour to see such buildings which were also illustrated in printed pattern books so that they could be copied.

Undoubtedly Standlynch would have been the weekend retreat of many, hosting gatherings of Dilletanti from London who would have luxuriated in the classical designs of the house and the picturesque beauty of the countryside.

The house was presented to the Nelson family in 1813 after the Battle of Trafalgar (1805) and renamed.[7] The family lived there until 1947 after which the house had several owners. It is now owned by Michael Wade and hosts weddings and concerts. The south wing was remodeled and is the venue for wedding receptions while the north wing is internally semi-derelict.

To the west of the old manor house and close to the river, a 'wilderness' area was given high walls on four sides and converted into a kitchen garden for the new house.

The new Standlynch Farm was built to the north-east of the old settlement, on the road connecting Downton and Witherington. The buildings are now called Old Standlynch Farm. The farmhouse (now called Standlynch House) dates from about 1733 and was extended considerably to the north in the late nineteenth century. There were two large corn barns which date from this time and several cottages and workshops which most probably followed reasonably quickly - one of these has graffiti 'HD 1777'.

The corn barns evidence the importance of cereal and sheep farming on the chalk downs, and the dominance of home-based agriculture before the abolition of the Corn Laws in 1846 eventually opened the domestic market to much cheaper imported grain and so signaled the end of mass grain growing in the UK.

The other new farm – the Standlynch Dairy Farm – was built in the late seventeenth century when the water meadows were created on the eastern bank of the Avon and were described as old in 1814 and derelict by 1975.[8]

A mill existed across part of the river in 1311 and is also mentioned in 1383 but not after that until 1575-6. A new mill and weir were built in the current location in 1697-8. In 1884 the mill housed an engine and pump to lift water to Trafalgar House, and this remained in use until 1907. In the 1940s it housed an electric generation plant for the Trafalgar Estate.

The first church was built around 1147 when permission was granted for a church, graveyard and priest's house. The church was to be a daughter church to that in Downton and was dedicated to St Mary. Clearly there was conflict between Downton and Standlynch and this arrangement lapsed in the 1300s when a chaplain was appointed and then withdrawn in 1399.

By the early seventeenth century the inhabitants of Standlynch were recusants and the church used for Catholic Masses. It became a private chapel

The part derelict church at Standlynch. The current structure was built in 1677 and then substantially restored and rebuilt by William Butterfield in 1859-66 (photograph John Elliott)

for the Bucklands who were the Lords of the Manor from the late sixteenth century. Their lands were sequestered and they were named as recusants around 1629. Walter Buckland received the Anglican sacrament in 1641 but suspicions remained that he was still a recusant, partly because he opposed Parliament during the Civil War. In 1646 he was obliged to receive the Anglican sacrament again. His wife and tenants remained openly Catholic and the church was most probably used for Masses until his son, Maurice, succeeded to the title and conformed to the Church of England. The current church was initially built in 1677.

After the Nelsons occupied Trafalgar House the Anglicanism continued and the church was also used by the residents of Charlton All Saints until a church was built in that village in 1851. The building was rebuilt again to the designs of William Butterfield in 1859-66.

It is a flint and ashlar stone structure, the stones and flints being laid in a chequer pattern. There is a chancel, nave, northern vestry and south-western porch. At this time the church must have been used for "High" Anglo-Catholic worship as there are memorials in the porch which link Standlynch with Wantage which was a major centre of such practices.

Things evolved further when the wife of Horatio, Earl Nelson, converted to Roman Catholicism in 1896. Thomas Nelson, who succeeded his father in 1913, was also a Roman Catholic and turned the church into a private chapel with a resident priest.[9] It was rededicated to Mary Queen of Angels and St Michael and all the Angels. The church remained active until the Nelson family left in 1947, at which point it was closed and a new Roman Catholic chapel was erected on the outskirts of Downton. The Standlynch church still stands but is semi derelict.

While it is now mostly noted for its scenic views, good walks and excellent, but exclusive, fishing, Standlynch was previously an important settlement between Salisbury and Downton, and the site of a major eighteenth century gentleman's house. Its geographic separation enabled it to exert an independence that might not have been available in a more populous area, and this was particularly notable in matters religious.[10] Trafalgar House survives and the area around it is farmed as a single unit rather than as subdivided units previously. While the future of the house and chapel may cause some concern the area's general future seems assured by its picturesqueness for living and by its mixed farming. Many refer to Trafalgar House in the same way as they pronounce the London Square of the same name. Others prefer instead to adopt a Spanish pronunciation that emphasizes the first and last syllables. Apparently the Nelson family preferred the latter.

Notes

1   See VCH ii, 119, 150-1, 161 & 208
2   VCH iv, 357
3   Standlynch with Charlton All Saints Parish. It joined the Alderbury poor-law union in 1835.
4   See *Country Life* 13 July 1945.
5   The interior of the north wing was replanned in the early nineteenth century and the south wing remodeled after a fire in 1866.
6   See *Vitruvius Britannicus* v, 1771, pls 78-81 and *Country Life* 13-20 July 1945.
7   Battle of Trafalgar 1805
8   Little remains today.
9   See *Daily Mail* 22 November 1913.
10 There is a comprehensive history of Standlynch in VCH xi, mostly, but not exclusively, on pages 68-72.

Starve or Set Sail:
Wiltshire Emigration to
Canada, 1830-1880

Lucille H Campey

Wiltshire emigration to Canada, which began in earnest during the 1830s, was driven by the great poverty being experienced by Wiltshire's farm labourers and Canada's need to attract loyal settlers. Having been invaded by American troops in 1812 there were concerns that Canada was vulnerable to further attacks from the United States. Sir John Colborne, the Lieutenant Governor of Upper Canada (later Ontario), believed that British settlers were urgently needed to act as a defensive buffer against the colony's largely American population whose loyalty to Britain was suspect. However, this was easier said than done. Few British people could afford the high cost of travelling to the vast inland stretches of mid-Canada and, in any case, there was a great deal of apprehension about the merits of emigration. Matters came to a head in rural England in the early 1830s when, with the spread of mechanisation, threshing machines arrived, throwing countless farm labourers out of work.

Led by the fictitious Captain Swing, rioting swept through the agricultural counties, with Wiltshire, Sussex, Kent and Norfolk being in the forefront of the disturbances. A debate raged over how public funds might be used to alleviate the humanitarian crisis. This led to the passing of The Poor Law Amendment Act of 1834; one of the most significant pieces of social legislation ever enacted. It allowed English parishes to raise funds locally for emigration schemes. They could make a one-off payment to fund their paupers' emigration costs. Their ratepayers were spared the burden of continuing poor relief costs while Canada acquired more settlers. Everybody won – at least in theory.

The parish of Corsley in west Wiltshire was one of the first to opt for assisted emigration, doing so in 1830, even before the new legislation had been enacted. It raised £300 to help sixty-six of its paupers to emigrate to Upper Canada. Included in their number was William Singer who could not wait to put pen to paper:

> If any of my old acquaintances is got tired of being slaves and drudges tell them to come to Upper Canada to William Singer and he will take them by the hand and lead them to hard work and good wages and the best of living. Any of them would do well here ... We have eight English families within about two miles all from Westbury or Corsley.[1]

Similarly, Philip Annett was also very upbeat:

> I think you was better sell your house and ... and come to Canada whilst you have a chance If you don't come soon it is likely you will starve and if you don't your children will ... I was agreeably surprised when I came here to see what a fine country it was – it being excellent land bearing crops of wheat and other corn for 20 or 30 years without any dung. You have no rent to pay, no poor-rates and scarcely any taxes. No gamekeepers or Lords over you ... I think no Englishman can do better than come as soon as possible, if it cost them every farthing they have, for I would rather be so here than in England with £100 in my pocket.[2]

Their buoyant aspirations can be contrasted with Maud Davies' unsympathetic view which she expressed in a village history nearly 80 years later:

> In 1830 the parish of Corsley, Wiltshire, shipped off at its own cost sixty six of the least desirable of its inhabitants, about half being adults and half children ...
>
> The emigrants consisted of several families of the very class one would wish to remove, men of suspected bad habits who brought up their children to wickedness, whilst there were several poachers amongst them, and other reputed bad characters.[3]

Far from being useless degenerates the Corsley immigrants grabbed the employment opportunities that were now available to them, thus sparking off a more or less immediate outflow of people from the neighbouring parishes of Frome in Somerset, and Horningsham and Westbury in Wiltshire. Between 1830 and 1832 the Corsley/Frome area lost around eight hundred poor people to Upper Canada, all of whom were assisted by their parishes.[4] A group from Frome, which left in 1831, had its departure described in the local newspaper:

> No influence was used ... everyone went entirely of his own free choice, with local people helping them with provisions and clothing; In the night of 21st March, 1831 eighty five men, women and children left with their baggage set out in seven carriages, preceded by a band of music. Three proper persons accompanied them to preserve order and attend to their wants ... The women were in tears at the thought of parting forever from their native country.'[5]

Highly favourable reports of Upper Canada, which were sent by the Frome immigrants to friends and family back home, were widely circulated,[6] and this in turn helped to stimulate the exodus of one hundred and fifty six paupers in the following year, many being related to people in the earlier group.[7] Their arrival at the port of Quebec was described – by no less a person than William Lyon Mackenzie, a prominent politician whose grandson would become Canada's longest serving Prime Minister:

> One afternoon I went onboard the ship *Airthy Castle* from Bristol, immediately after her arrival. The passengers were in number two hundred and fifty four, all in the hold or steerage; all English, from about Bristol, Bath, Frome, Warminster, Maiden Bradley, etc.. I went below and truly it was a curious sight. Over two hundred human beings, male and female, young old and middle-aged, talking, singing, laughing, crying, eating, drinking, shaving, washing, some naked in bed, and others dressing to go on shore; handsome young women (perhaps some) and ugly old men, married and single; religious and irreligious ... These settlers were poor, but in general they were fine-looking people and such as I was glad to see come to America ... It is my opinion that few among them will forget being cooped up below deck for four weeks in a moveable bedroom with

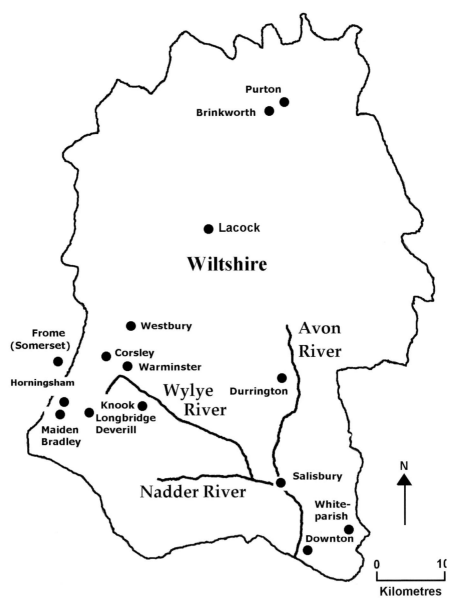

Parishes in Wiltshire and Somerset from which people were assisted to emigrate to Upper Canada, 1830–1940

two hundred and fifty fellow-lodgers as I have endeavoured to describe.[8]

Forty paupers from the Lacock estate also relocated to Upper Canada in 1832, having been assisted by William Henry Fox Talbot, their landlord. According to Henrietta Fielding, his half-sister, the estate was well rid of them: 'Mr Paley [the Vicar] says they remind him of the 40 thieves! – but so much the better riddance … Mama has given clothes to the women, 10 of whom are going.'[9] Lady Fielding, Fox Talbot's mother, thought it wise not to give them anything 'till the last moment otherwise, Mr. Spencer tells me, they are likely to sell it.'[10] Despite this negative assessment of their worth, the Lacock paupers would go on to enrich Canada's population and greatly improve their own prospects. Because they could sell their labour to the highest bidder in Canada's classless society, they would earn considerably higher wages than the pittances they were paid in Lacock.

The Wiltshire and Somerset paupers were initially sent to Peterborough and Simcoe counties, on the north side of Lake Ontario, in the hope that they would supplement the long-established American communities along the lake frontage. Mary Sophia (Gapper) O'Brien, from Charlinch in Somerset, came upon their communities when she visited in the 1830s:

> Now for the first time I saw quite a new settlement. We passed on
> for two miles through a road just cut out on each side of which
> at short intervals were log houses of a very respectable class.
> Some were finished externally but almost all stood completely

This pencil drawing by Titus Ware Hibbert of a Log House in Simcoe County in 1844 provides an artist's impression of the scene described by Mary O'Brien. Toronto Public Library

in the forest. In some places there was perhaps an acre or two chopped, but generally hardly so many trees seemed to have fallen as were necessary to construct the buildings … In five or six years every house will be surrounded by a productive farm. Most of these settlers are farmers from England.[11]

The Lake Erie region, much further to the west, also acquired Wiltshire and Somerset paupers; but their location was determined by local knowledge, not the dictates of the Canadian government. Good intelligence had come from Joseph Silcox, a Corsley man who had worked as a glazier and was also a Congregational minister. Having emigrated at his own expense to the Lake Erie region in 1817, he had been followed by friends and family. Described as 'a ragged Christian of the Calvinist type with an iron frame who made the forest resound with both his axe and his exhortations,' Silcox was a remarkable leader. The good land in the region contributed to the group's rapid success and before long most of the west Wiltshire and Somerset families, who had been assisted by their parishes to emigrate, ended up in the Lake Erie region. The Frome that sprouted near St. Thomas and the Corsley which appeared a short distance away became living reminders of transferred Wiltshire origins.[12]

Meanwhile, the disastrous economic conditions that had afflicted the Corsley/Frome area were also being experienced in Downton parish on the south east side of the county. In addition to the plight of the male farm labourers, women and girls had lost their lace making jobs to machines, thus denying their families much-needed supplementary income.

Once again emigration was seized upon as the solution and in 1835 the parish paid the expenses of twenty five Downton people. The group spent five nights at the Quebec Hotel in Portsmouth Harbour while they awaited a favourable wind to take their ship westward to Quebec. Records of their food and drinks bills reveal that the Downton people enjoyed sumptuous meals washed down with copious quantities of ale, port and other alcoholic beverages. Breakfasts with lobster, mackerel or steak were followed in the evening by salmon, steak, lamb cutlets or lamb chops. The drinks bill for their last night, amounting to 7s. 8d, was roughly the average weekly wage of an agricultural labourer![13] The inescapable conclusion is that fine food and drink had been offered to apprehensive people to allay their fears of what lay ahead. It would seem that the strategy worked. After a non-eventful crossing their early reports were highly favourable, this being typical:

You told me that we should repent of coming to Canada, and surely we do, but it is because we did not come before … This I have to say, that any labouring man can live better by working three days a week than at home by working all of the week … Here are no poor-rates, for there are no poor here.[14]

With this sort of endorsement many more followed. Some two hundred and twenty people from Downton and fifty nine from Whiteparish sailed to Quebec in 1836, most relocating to the Lake Erie region, becoming near neighbours of the Corsley and Frome settlers described earlier.[15] Paupers from Longbridge Deverill, Durrington, Purton and Brinkworth also left for Upper Canada in the 1830s and 1840s but by then the number of Wiltshire people being assisted to emigrate by their parishes had greatly reduced.[16] This was also the time when a small group from Devizes founded a New Wiltshire in Prince Edward Island on the east side of Canada.[17]

The clamour for assisted emigration increased once again in the 1870s, a time when rising cheap food imports from abroad contributed to the miserable plight of labourers. Having a chronic shortage of farm workers Ontario sent its agents to rural England in the hope of capitalizing on the increasing zeal to emigrate. They extolled the merits of Ontario's huge agricultural potential and, as an added enticement, the British and Ontario

'Downton Daisy', a Downton lace sample made in the 19th century. Downton had two lace-making schools in 1819. Salisbury and South Wiltshire Museum

governments made funds available to help with the cost of sea crossings while English agricultural trade unions also offered their support.

When George T. Denison, the Ontario Immigration Commissioner toured Wiltshire from his base in Salisbury in 1873 he attracted enthusiastic and well-attended gatherings of farm workers. Although local trade union leaders helped him to organize the various meetings, some farmers voiced their disapproval, fearing that emigration would increase the wages of the labourers who remained. 'Often the clergymen, who have control of the venues, refuse to hire them or let them be used for emigration lectures.' Occasionally he had to speak 'in the open air to the poor labourers [either] in the street or village green'.[18] However, by 1880 trade union leaders withdrew their support, realizing that assisting labourers to emigrate meant that their most able members were being lost to Canada. Afterwards the poor had to rely more on their own initiative and on help they could muster from their parishes, landlords and philanthropic bodies.

The relocation of thousands of Wiltshire's poor to Canada in the 1830s and 1840s gave mid-Canada's farming population a much needed boost. Canada benefitted from their farming skills and experience, while they escaped from their poverty. In their letters home many revealed how they were offered work soon after arriving – some while waiting for their luggage to arrive! These humble labourers, who came with little apart from a determination to succeed, played a vital role in Canada's early development. However, they left few outward signs of their Englishness behind, simply fading into the background and becoming Canadians.

Notes

1   George Poullett Scrope, 1831, *Extracts of Letters from Poor Persons Who Emigrated Last Year to Canada and the United States for the Information of the Labouring Poor in this Country*, J. Ridgeway, 28–9

2   *Ibid,* 11–2, 14–5

3   Maud Frances Davies, 1909, *Life in an English Village: An Economic and Historical Survey of the Parish of Corsley in Wiltshire*, T. Fisher Unwin

4   Lucille H. Campey, 2012, *Seeking a Better Future: The English Pioneers of Ontario and Quebec*, Dundurn, 132–7

5   Somerset Record Office (hereafter SRO) DD/SF/4546: Sanford family papers, Anonymous letter published in *Bath and Cheltenham Gazette, 28th March, 1831* entitled 'Emigration from Frome to Canada'.

6   SRO T\PH\SAS/8/925/1J: O. Lewis, 1945, *Letters from Poor Persons who Emigrated to Canada from the Parish of Frome in the County of Somerset,* Frome Newspaper Co Ltd

7   SRO DD\LW/49: Frome Vestry Book, 1815–1878

8   William Lyon Mackenzie, 1833, *Sketches of Canada and the United States,* 179–81

9   British Library, Fox Talbot Papers: Henrietta Fielding to William Henry Fox Talbot, 8th May, 1832

10 *Ibid,* Elizabeth Fielding to Fox Talbot, 7th May, 1832

11 Audrey Saunders Miller (ed), 1968, *The Journals of Mary O'Brien,* Macmillan of Canada, 152-3

12 Corsley was later renamed Sheddon. For a description of Wiltshire and Somerset emigration to the Lake Erie region see Campey, *Seeking a Better Future,* 162-8

13 Wiltshire and Swindon Archives (hereafter WSA) 1306/105: Downton parish, receipts for money paid on behalf of the 1835 group.

14 The letter writer was anonymous. David Waymouth,1999, *Downton, 7,000 years of an English Village,* Cromwell Press, 133

15 Campey, *Seeking a Better Future,* 170-3

16 WSA 1020/55 Longbridge Deverill Vestry Minute Book; WSA 306/66, 212B/5644: Purton emigration papers; WSA 1607/64, 1607/71 Brinkworth Vestry Book. Poor Law Commissioners, 1836, *The Second Annual Report of the Poor Law Commissioners for England and Wales,* HMSO, 571-4

17 Lucille H. Campey, 2010, *Planters, Paupers and Pioneers: English Settlers in Atlantic Canada,* Dundurn, 184, 363

18 Ontario Archives F1009 MU1724: George T. Denison fonds (letter book), 35–65

Victorian Banburyshire: Three Memoirs

Edited by Barry Trinder, *Banbury Historical Society* Vol 33 2013

One of the three memoirs in this volume (the others are from Thomas Ward Boss 1825–1903, and Thomas Butler Gunn 1863) comes from Sarah Beesley who lived from 1812 to 1900. She published *My Life* in a small edition in 1892, based on correspondence and diaries kept during many decades. Amongst much of interest are reports of two visits to Salisbury, reproduced here. Her husband Thomas Beesley was an amateur geologist and archaeologist of some distinction. He made some significant discoveries studying the geology revealed in quarries and railway cuttings around Banbury, and had a wide acquaintance with eminent scientists in the field, referred to by Sarah in the final sentence from her 1874 visit quoted below. The Beesleys' son Thomas (b 1846) received a somewhat chequered education, including a spell at Queenwood College, Tytherley, which specialised in innovative science teaching. He spent time in his father's chemist shop, and passed his first pharmaceutical examination in 1868. In 1873 he set up his own business in Salisbury, recorded in 1875 Kelly's *Directory* as 'chemist and druggist' at 10 High Street. Tom Beesley married Mattie Spinney, who lived at 52 Endless Street, in St Edmund's church on 9 October 1873. Her father was Thomas Edward Spinney, 'professor of music and organist of the parish church of Wilton'. Five years later Tom and Mattie left Salisbury to start a business in Clapham, London. In 1886 Tom became dispenser at Westminster Hospital.

1874

Sarah [*daughter b 1848*] and I spent nearly a fortnight with my son Tom at Salisbury, leaving Banbury on the 18th of June, and returning on the 30th.

This was my first visit to Salisbury, and I was very much struck with the beautiful Cathedral with its lofty spire, the churches, the curious Poultry Cross, the old houses with their upper storeys hanging over the pavement, etc.

We paid an early visit to the magnificent Cathedral. It is built in the form of a double cross, extending in its extreme dimensions, from west to east, 473 feet, and from north to south – the length of the principal transept – 229 feet 7 inches. The great elevation of its graceful spire renders it the most lofty in the kingdom, being about 400 feet from the ground.

There are many monuments in the Cathedral, which would be very interesting to an archaeologist, I have no doubt. The nave is lofty, though somewhat narrow; and the transepts, like the nave, rise to an elevation of three storeys. Over the entrance to each of the transepts are two Perpendicular arches, which were inserted early in the fifteenth century by way of counter-thrust against the weight of the central tower.

I was very much pleased both with the exterior and the interior of the cathedral, and went into the Cathedral Close to have a good view of it. The building stands displayed on all sides, and is surrounded by green turf, intersected with neat gravel walks, and tastefully planted with rows and avenues of fine trees.

There is a very large Market Place at Salisbury, and near to it is the famous Poultry Cross, which I saw and admired.

We visited the Halle of John Halle, which is now used as a china dealer's showroom, and made several purchases. This lofty banqueting room was built by John Halle, an eminent woolstapler, who flourished in the reigns of Henry VI and Edward VI. High up on the walls are busts of angels holding shields and lower down hang some portraits. The windows are very large and are of stained glass. There is a large oak screen or cabinet at one end of the hall, the carvings and figures of which are very elaborate and curious.

The Museum is very interesting and includes one of the largest series of flint and stone implements in the kingdom. Much care has been taken to illustrate the habits and practices of bygone races, in regards to their weapons and ornaments by bringing similar specimens in use among modern savages at a very recent period side by side with those obtained from tumuli, caves etc. I saw the names of geologists whom I had seen at Banbury on some of the collections.

[*They also went to Wilton House, Stonehenge and Winchester during this visit*]

1877

In the summer of this year Bessie [*daughter b 1850*] and I paid a visit of more than a fortnight's duration to Salisbury. [*23rd July – 7 August*]

We paid another visit to the Halle of John Halle and the Museum, which I found much improved since my former visit. We did not forget the Cathedral. This was still undergoing repair, as it was on our former visit, and had been since 1863. We heard the grand organ. The organist had to go up a ladder at that time to play it. Six men are required to blow the bellows.

Tom and Mattie spent a few days at a pretty house about a mile from Salisbury called 'Elm Grove', and we had a pleasant day there with Mattie's father and mother. There are some beautiful and extensive views from this house. We saw Laverstock Church and the Asylum. One of the inmates of the Asylum who passed us was pointed out to me as the son of Lord Napier.

Jane Howells

A 19th century workhouse scandal

Ruth Newman

In June 1856 the *Salisbury Journal* announced that an 'important inquest' had taken place at the city workhouse into the death of a young child. The tragedy of an innocent victim 'excited great interest in the city' at the time and was to have significant repercussions.[1]

The Poor Law in Salisbury - background

The problems of poverty, unemployment and poor relief first threatened to overwhelm Salisbury in the early 17th century, partly because of a contraction in markets for the woollen cloth industry at home and

Salisbury workhouse, Crane Street, west range,
©Peter Higginbotham/workhouses.org.uk

Salisbury workhouse, Crane Street, south range; built in 1728 as an enlargement to the workhouse. It housed the workshop with dormitories above, © Peter Higginbotham/ workhouses.org.uk

overseas.[2] Despite considerable help from the almshouses, the three parishes, St Thomas's, St Edmund's and St Martin's, provided most of the relief for the city's poor. These were given assistance either in their own homes (out relief) or in the Crane Street workhouse. This 15th century building had been established as a workhouse in 1637 and served the city until 1879, originally housing just sixteen boys and fourteen girls 'not beinge Bastards'.[3] It was a conventional poor-house, far removed from the progressive Puritan schemes of the early 17th century.[4] A south range was added in 1728 which housed the workshop with dormitories above.[5]

In the first half of the 19th century the city experienced religious and political upheaval, agricultural 'Swing' riots [6] and one of the worst cholera outbreaks in the country in 1849.[7] These were troubled times for Salisbury following the long wars against France and by 1800 the poor relief system, including the workhouse, was increasingly criticised, simply unable to cope with the sheer number of those in distress. With over 2000 in poverty in the city the poor rates had risen more than four times between 1780 and 1800 and were the largest area of local expenditure. As such, they met opposition from the rate payers.[8] Henry Wansey, a Warminster clothier, living in Salisbury, in a damning report of 1801, described the workhouse as inefficiently managed and overcrowded. In his *Thoughts on Poor Houses* he offered a mixture of practical suggestions and economies to save on the rates. He recommended that inmates should be made to work, weekly visits and reports undertaken by paid officials, and children kept separate and given an education. More vegetables should be grown to save on the expense of meat and he included a little personal eulogy on the benefits of parsnips which could save the workhouse £300 a year. The paupers were simply eating and drinking too well. [9]

Many of his findings were endorsed by the 1834 Poor Law Report. Assistant Commissioner Okeden wrote that 'he had never seen a more disgusting scene of filth and misrule than the Salisbury Workhouse.'[10] The subsequent Act combined parishes into Unions under elected Boards of Guardians and established the 'well regulated' workhouse to act as a deterrent, believing that only the genuinely desperate would apply for relief.[11]

The three city parishes had already joined together by an Act of 1770

Salisbury workhouse courtyard looking west, showing 15th century range, Grundy Heape 1934

to share rates and administer relief.[12] Despite criticism, they remained as a 'Union' with their own Board of Guardians, in the workhouse in Crane Street, largely exempt from the terms of the 1834 Act. A new Alderbury Union workhouse at the junction of the Coombe/Odstock roads, south of the city, was built in 1836, as a direct result of the Poor Law Amendment Act. Accommodating up to 200 paupers from the Close and 21 other local parishes including Fisherton and Milford, it incorporated many of the strict 'rules' laid down in 1834: segregation of men, women and children, compulsory uniform and mindless jobs like stone breaking. Local rates fell so the new system was deemed a success.[13]

The city workhouse in Crane Street continued to receive a bad press. Thomas Rammell's Report on the sanitary condition of Salisbury 1851, following the cholera outbreak just two years earlier, described the workhouse as 'unfitting' with an open privy and 'very defective as to ventilation'. Four deaths were recorded from cholera.[14]

The workhouse, 1856

It was against this background of increasing criticism that the 1856 scandal broke. It was reported in the *Salisbury Journal* that nine year old Louisa (Sophia) Garrett had died at the workhouse on the 5 June, shortly after being taken out of a sulphur bath, used 'for the cure of persons afflicted with the itch'.[15] Even the christian name of the young pauper girl seemed uncertain, compounding the tragedy.[16] The inquest was held two days later. The jury, having examined the bath, noted that it had been used without medical supervision as was regular practice in other local poor law unions such as Devizes. The girl had been left immersed for at least 35 minutes.[17] She called for water, went black in the face and died shortly after. The medical officer of the workhouse, Dr John Winzar [18] confirmed that the child had died from being left too long in the contraption (ten minutes were sufficient). He also complained that the workhouse master should have told him of its presence in the building. The post mortem concluded that the child had died from 'congestion of the brain' and the jury, 'after long deliberation', concurred, also condemning the blocks of wood used to raise the child. [19]

The case, with the tragic death of a young child, was reported to the Poor Law Commissioners in London. Action followed rapidly; the next week an investigation was announced with an inspector sent from the Poor Law Board.[20] The Inquiry began at the Salisbury Workhouse on 19 June with full details, as follows, from the press report, provided by the *Salisbury Journal*.[21]

W H T Hawley was a Poor Law inspector for Wilts, Hants and Dorset and was sent to Salisbury by the central board, such was the gravity of the 'accident'. The Mayor, several representatives from the Board of Guardians and some of the jurymen from the inquest were present.

The investigation provides a fascinating account of workhouse life in the mid 19th century. Thomas Jeans, the master, who had been in this position almost 13 years, was the first witness. He reported that 'cutaneous' (skin) diseases were not uncommon especially among the children and the frequency of the infection had increased recently. Sulphur ointment had been applied but was largely ineffective but he believed that the sulphur bath was used to good effect in the Devizes Union and was the 'most efficient method of curing itch'. A full description of its use, given by Jeans, with horrifying details, is worth recounting. 'It is a kind of box, with an opening for the head ... perfectly air tight ... The way to use it is this:- Get a pan with a little clear fire, throw some powdered sulphur over it; place it . . . under the perforated seat [in the bath]. . . Then place your patient in the chair naked, shut it up, and fill the space where the neck comes through with wet sheet, and keep up a good fire for about an hour. Take the patient out, wrap in blankets, and when the redness caused by the sulphur is gone off, look if the spots are dead and appear dull; if so, a warm bath, . . . a clean suit of clothes, and the itch is gone'.[22]

Following advice from Mr Hassell, the Devizes master, a bath was ordered for the workhouse. The porter attended the males, the schoolmistress stayed with the females. It was not considered necessary to notify the Medical Officer and Mr Jeans believed it 'perfectly safe' and 'would have submitted my own children to it'. From the start some of the jurymen asked searching questions especially about the role of John Winzar. The inspector had to call them to order reminding them that 'they were here to see whether the child died through neglect' not to ask 'improper' questions. It appeared that although the medical officer had recommended the bath he had not actually seen it in use.

Mrs Jeans, the matron was then sworn in.[23] She was present when Sophia was placed in the bath, following two other girls who suffered no ill effects. Miss Wheeler, the industrial teacher, was to hand the whole time, but when Mrs Jeans returned 'a change' had come over Sophia and when taken from the bath 'appeared quite dead'.

The inquiry then cross examined the medical officer himself. John Winzar confirmed that the 'itch' was a long running problem especially among the children. He agreed that in April he had recommended the 'occasional use of sulphur baths' but was not 'aware of its adoption until I was called in to see the deceased'. He did not know the girl or whether

her weak constitution should have precluded her from the contraption but understood it to be successful in Devizes. He was questioned vigourously about his attendance and it was suggested that he had not 'visited the house for sixteen weeks' and had fabricated entries in the medical book after the tragedy had occurred. Winzar denied this and a heated argument followed – 'a grosser fabrication could not issue from man's mouth' was his accusation to Mr Rooke, the juryman.[24] The inspector repeated that he was not present to 'institute a general inquiry into the conduct of Mr Winzar'.

Mr Lush, the surgeon[25] who had performed the post mortem examination, found the 'body studded with spots' (the itch); 'on opening the skull I found the brain loaded with blood'. He confirmed that it was his conclusion that the girl had died 'by a too lengthened action of the vapour of the sulphur bath . . . I should consider 40 minutes too long for a girl of that description' ('a fat, heavy child, with a short neck and plump features'). He also believed that there should be proper medical superintendence since most children vomited. Mr Rooke persisted; 'If she had not been in the bath she would have been alive now?' – (Lush) 'most decidedly'. Mr Rooke – 'the bath was the death of her'. The inspector, at this point, appeared anxious to protect John Winzar whose views on the efficacy of the bath differed from surgeon Lush who wished to restrict its use.

Louisa Wheeler, the industrial schoolmistress[26] was the next witness who was subject to detailed cross examination. She was with Sophia during her time in the bath and acted as supervisor, reporting that many children

The Alderbury, later Salisbury Union workhouse, photo courtesy of Peter Goodhugh

vomited and all asked to come out early. Sophia Garrett 'appeared the strongest and healthiest looking child in the house'. She asked for water, wanted to visit 'the closet and I told her that if she was a good girl she should come out'. After about 30 minutes 'she made a noise resembling snoring. She looked rather purple ... (and) fell out of the bath on its being opened. She was quite senseless and motionless ... The wood upon which she sat was covered with a dirty chemise.'

More interrogation followed, not only of the schoolmistress but of two female inmates, one of whom reported that Wheeler had hit the girl 'three or four times on the head with her open hand - not in anger but merely to rouse her'. The witness, Charlotte Sainsbury, was asked if she felt that she should have gone for assistance when the girl first appeared unwell but replied that she 'was ordered not to leave the place'.

Further difficult questions, increasingly acrimonious, were asked about the possibility of suppression of evidence or even of trying to prevent the inquiry taking place. Why had Joseph Hibberd, the town clerk, met the inspector for two hours at the *White Hart*? Equally strong denials followed – 'no attempt had been made to influence (the inspector) by Mr Hibberd who had come from the Board of Guardians'.

Mr Rooke concluded that it was a 'most cruel case', but the inspector repeated the known success of the bath and that 'it had never been thought necessary to have a medical man in consequence of the appliance being so simple' but perhaps in the future, especially with children, this might be advisable. The inquiry was declared closed with the proviso that the 'persons who were interested would soon hear from the Poor Law Board on the matter'.[27]

The *Salisbury Journal* produced no further details or results of the inquiry. Unfortunately the records from 1834-1864 for the Salisbury workhouse and its Board of Guardians' minutes no longer survive and with these sources not available, The National Archives filled in some of the missing details. The entire correspondence exists relating to the pauper girl, Sophia Garrett; a 19 page letter from the inspector to the Poor Law Board, letters from the coroner, statements from the workhouse master, matron, and the medical officer together with copies of the commissioners' replies. A letter written to the Board, even before the inquest, by the juryman James Rooke, demanded 'your most serious consideration' into the 'inhumane' death of the young girl 'whose life was sacrificed ... through the negligence of the medical officer of this city.' [28] The whole correspondence is a goldmine for local historians.

The central board's report was critical of John Winzar in that he did not know his patients, did not visit regularly, had never seen sulphur administered, did not inspect the sulphur bath and was 'remiss in the discharge of his duties . . . and deserves a severe reprimand for his negligence'. A letter written on 17 July from the Poor Law Board to Winzar requested that 'in future your Medical Relief book may be kept in strict accordance with the form prescribed' with a written certificate for the sulphur bath and the time prescribed. Further, the catastrophe was attributed to the failure of the Medical Officer to carry out his duties and to the ignorance of the workhouse officials. This was followed by an official reprimand both of John Winzar and of the schoolmistress who was in charge on the day. Wheeler had refused the child water, not recognised her severe distress, and used a cane to try to rouse her, the latter described as 'highly reprehensible'. It was agreed that the bath could still be used and the beneficial results were cited, but only for 15 minutes and only with the sanction of the Medical Officer in every case. It was the abuse of the bath that had caused the tragedy. [29] None of this was published in the local paper, a case perhaps of safeguarding the reputation of a well known medical figure in the city.

In an interesting sequel, juryman Mr Rooke wrote several times to the Poor Law Board demanding, as a rate payer, to see a copy of the report of the inquiry which had been sent to the church wardens and overseers of the city. The Board bypassed responsibility stating that publication was at the discretion of the church wardens who then failed to release the report. As late as 5 September, Mr Rooke stated that he had been 'positively refused' access. After repeated delays, the details of the report and a copy of the letter to John Winzar were forwarded to the Coroner, and the persistent juryman fighting for the rights of a pauper child, was able to see the official reprimand of the surgeon John Winzar. [30]

Further criticism led to the demise of the Crane Street Workhouse. The Salisbury and Alderbury Unions amalgamated in 1869 and a new enlarged workhouse for 400 paupers was built in 1877-1879 on the Coombe Road site. The earlier Alderbury workhouse seems to have been demolished and a new infirmary built in its place. The inmates from Crane Street moved in 1880 to their new 'home', renamed officially the Salisbury Union Workhouse in 1895. The buildings, apart from the much altered Victorian chapel, currently the Harnham Free Church, were largely demolished in the 1970s to be replaced by the Ridings Mead housing estate. [31]

After 242 years the city workhouse in Crane Street finally closed in 1879. The building was purchased by the Church of England and restored by the architect George Crickmay [32] and in 2014, as *Church House*, contains the administrative offices of the Salisbury Diocese.

Bibliography & Abbreviations

SJ = *Salisbury and Winchester Journal*

RCHME= Royal Commission on the Historical Monuments of England, 1980, *City of Salisbury,* HMSO

VCH = *Victoria County History of Wiltshire,* volumes V & VI

TNA = *The National Archives*

WSA = *Wiltshire and Swindon Archives*

Newman, R & Howells, J, 2001, *Salisbury Past,* Phillimore

Rammell, Thomas W, 1851, *Report of the General Board of Health on a preliminary inquiry into the sewerage, drainage and supply of water, and the sanitary condition of the inhabitants of the city and borough of Salisbury, in the county of Wilts.* London: HMSO

Slack, P, 1975, *Poverty in Early-Stuart Salisbury, Wiltshire Record Society* XXXI

Wansey, Henry, 1801, *Thoughts on Poor-Houses, with a view to their general reform, as applicable to Salisbury.* London: Cadell

Notes

1   I am grateful to Sue Johnson for initially alerting me to the *Salisbury Journal's* report on the workhouse tragedy. *SJ,* 07 June 1856, 3

2   Newman, & Howells, 41-44

3   VCH, VI, 111; Slack, Paul, 13; WSA G23/1/107

4   Slack, Paul, 1975, ibid, 9- 14 *passim*: Newman & Howells, ibid, 45-46

5   RCHME, *City of Salisbury,* 73

6   The Swing riots of the autumn of 1830 were agricultural uprisings, particularly severe in the Salisbury area. The underlying causes were low wages in the poverty stricken rural south but the immediate target of the labourers was the threshing machines which took away the guaranteed winter work of hand threshing.

7   Newman, Ruth, 2006, 'Salisbury in the Age of Cholera', *Sarum Chronicle* 6, 11-19

8   VCH, VI, 111

9   Wansey, *passim*

10   *Poor Law commission Report* (1834), App A, Pt I, 8a-9a; VCH 5, 253, note 60

11   Poor Law Amendment Act (1834): Newman & Howells, ibid 78

12   In 1770 the three Salisbury parishes were united under a local Act of Parliament to administer poor relief. This was to prevent St Thomas's, the wealthiest parish, from breaking away; www.workhouses.org.uk/Salisbury/(accessed 2014)

13   Newman & Howells, ibid 78; www.workhouses.org.uk/Alderbury/(accessed 2014)

14   Rammell, 13-15

15   *SJ,* 07 June 1856, p3; sulphur springs were long been recognised for their therapeutic properties in treating skin conditions. Suphur ointment had been used to treat 'the itch' (probably a form of scabies) before the use of the sulphur bath. It was stressed at the inquiry that it was not the amount of the sulphur powder that was at fault but the time of the immersion. No particular quantity of sulphur was used, the directions being 'to keep up a good fume'.

16   The first report (07 June) in the *Salisbury Journal* referred to 'Louisa'. By 21 June 'Louisa' had become 'Sophia' and the 1851 census confirms that this was her correct

name. In that year she was living, aged four, at Milford with her parents and two brothers. Her father, William was a postmaster, (HO107;1847,f18). At the inquest five years later he is described as a former 'fly-master (coach master) of this city'. What particular tragedy had led young Sophia to be in the workhouse has been impossible to trace.

17 The bath was described as a large box with a hole in the lid for the head. Sophia, because she was a child, had to be placed on two pieces of wood to keep her at the required height and to prevent strangulation. Wet cloths were placed over the hole to stop the sulphur fumes escaping.

18 John Winzar (1805-76) was well known in Salisbury's 19th century medical history. Often a controversial figure, he wrote in *Vital statistics of the city of Salisbury* (1849),that the water channels were effective for 'carrying away the sewage of the city' while others were pressing for their total abolition. Quoted in VCH VI, 114

19 *SJ,* 07 June 1856, p3

20 *SJ,* 14 June 1856, p3

21 *SJ,* 21 June 1856, p4

22 Thomas Jeans, the workhouse master, was an experienced official and remained in his post for nearly 30 years. He was later exonerated by the Poor Law Board of all blame 'having acted as he believed under the directions of this Board'. TNA Corres. 1834-1869 [MH 12/13847] (Salisbury)

23 The matron, Mrs Jeans, was in fact probably Grace Jeans, the unmarried sister of the workhouse master. She had previously been a teacher at Wilton workhouse, where her mother was matron. It appears that she was given the courtesy title 'Mrs' Jeans because of her position of authority as matron. The verdict on Mrs Jeans' role was 'unblameable'. Howells, J, 2007, *Independent women in public life in Salisbury in the second half of the nineteenth century,* unpublished PhD thesis, Goldsmiths, University of London; TNA Corres. 1834-1869 [MH 12/13847] (Salisbury)

24 In correspondence with the Poor Law Board James Lewis Rooke is described as an auctioneer and valuer living in New Street; TNA Corres. 1834-1869 [MH 12/13847] (Salisbury)

25 Dr John Alfred Lush (1815-88) was in private practice in Salisbury and later joined his brother-in –law, Dr Finch, on the management staff at Fisherton House Asylum eventually becoming proprietor. He was Mayor in 1867 and Liberal MP for the city from 1868-80. As President of the Medico-Psychological Association he became a noted expert on the care of the insane: *bjp.rcpsych.org/content/34/147/471.1.full.pdf* (accessed 2014)

26 The schoolmistress, Louisa Wheeler was described at the inquest as an 'industrial woman' who taught the female children glove making and 'other industrial pursuits'. She resigned from her post on 9 October after the official report.

27 *SJ,* 21 June 1856, p4

28 TNA Corres. 1834-1869 [MH 12/13847] (Salisbury)

29 MH12 at The National Archives contains 16,741 volumes of correspondence. Regional projects are underway to make this material more accessible, including digitisation and indexing, not (yet) including this area (the nearest is Southampton). Anyone thinking of tackling this material at TNA is recommended to read *Living the Poor Life: a guide to the Poor Law Union Correspondence 1834-1871, held at the*

National Archives, Paul Carter and Natalie Whistance, 2011, British Association for Local History, which includes an insert explaining how to find MH12 contents in the new Discovery catalogue.

30 Letters from Mr Rooke, 23 July, 5 September; TNA Corres. 1834–1869 [MH 12/13847] (Salisbury)

31 www.workhouses.org.uk/Alderbury/(accessed 2014)

32 Royal Commission on the Historical Monuments of England, 1980, *City of Salisbury*, HMSO, 73

An Early Map of Amesbury

John Chandler

Historians and topographers of Amesbury have reason to be grateful to Henry Flitcroft (1697-1769) for his superb atlas of much of the parish, including the town, which was commissioned by the 3rd duke of Queensberry and surveyed in 1726.[1] His work is well known and has been used extensively.[2] Previously unnoticed, however, so far as I am aware, is a manuscript plan and survey dated 1748, by the Hampshire cartographer William Godson, which is included in a volume of similar maps among the Winchester city muniments now in Hampshire Archives.[3] It depicts the

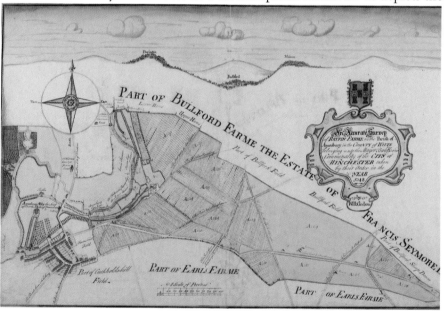

William Godson's map of Ratfyn and Amesbury, 1748 (HA W/F 5/1)

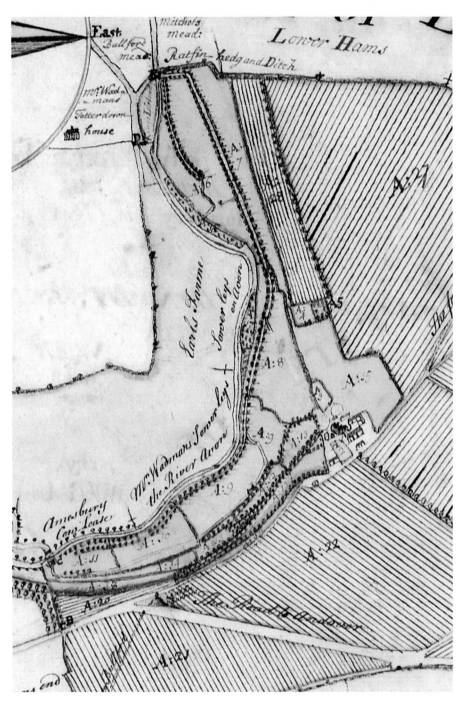

Detail of Godson's map, showing Ratfyn Farm and water meadows

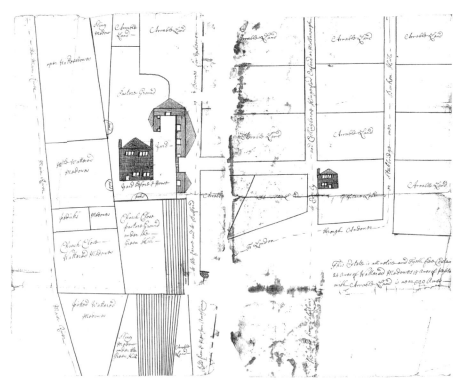

Rough sketch of Ratfyn farm, undated (WSA 1953/68)

settlement and fields of Ratfyn, in the north-east of the parish (now mostly lying astride the modern A303), but includes also a detailed plan of the town. Godson's map is interesting, I suggest, for four principal reasons. First, it portrays some 480 acres of Amesbury parish which were not surveyed by Flitcroft. Second, it offers a comparison, not only with Flitcroft's map of the town area, but also with a damaged and undated 18th-century sketch plan of the Ratfyn estate in Wiltshire & Swindon Archives.[4] Third, because it offers tiny perspective sketches of buildings and other features (unlike Flitcroft, which shows buildings in plan only) it depicts, albeit impressionistically, the appearance of the early Georgian town, which can be set against a detailed survey dated 1741 of some of its properties.[5] Finally it records the positions of several downland barrows on the slope of Beacon Hill which I suggest are not otherwise recorded.

Ratfyn, although a constituent of Amesbury parish since the middle ages, stood somewhat aloof from the rest until it joined the Antrobus lands in 1841. A Domesday estate, it was granted to endow a prebend in Old and then New Sarum Cathedral before *c* 1115, and had its own chapel of ease. In 1562 it was acquired by St John's Hospital, Winchester, an ancient foundation administered by the city corporation.[6] In the 18th century Ratfyn was a single farm held by tenants, or their sub-tenants, on renewable 21-year leases from the city fathers, who demanded not only £120 rent annually, but also a couple of turkeys or 5s in lieu each Christmas, and one night's entertainment for up to eight persons and their horses every fourth year, or £5 in lieu, when they came to inspect their property.[7] The lessees, members of a family named Lewis from before 1720, changed in 1749, when Ann Bulkeley of Burgate (Hants) became the absentee tenant. Her successor, James Blatch in 1770, was the resident yeoman farmer, and it was probably during his tenure that the present farmhouse was built.[8]

The 1748 Ratfyn map, measuring within its border 72 x 47cm, and drawn to a scale of 100 perches = 9cm. (1: 5589),[9] was the work of William Godson, at some time land surveyor to Winchester Corporation, but about whose life little else appears to be known.[10] He is celebrated in Winchester, however, for a very fine engraved map of the city dated 1750,[11] similar in ambition to William Naish's map of Salisbury, which (perhaps not coincidentally) was reissued in the following year. By comparison the Ratfyn map is somewhat crudely drawn; the individual character of the buildings is, with few exceptions, not captured and there is even a crossing-out and correction near the south-east corner. Accompanying the map is a survey giving names, land use and quantities (by two measures) of each land parcel, and totals of each category of use. The arable totalled 216 acres, and a further 58 acres of downland had been ploughed, leaving 167 acres of downland pasture. The remainder was water meadow (27 acres) and small acreages of enclosed and common pasture, osier beds and the farmstead. Fieldnames are unremarkable, although Church Mead (A9) and Church Close (A19) perhaps indicate that the medieval chapel lay west of the farm complex. William Cobbett, who described Ratfyn church as standing in the 1820s, had evidently lost his whereabouts, since only the name remained in 1748.[12] Burrow Field (A22) must refer to the still impressive Ratfyn Barrow (and perhaps its erstwhile neighbours), which is prominently drawn in one corner of the plot.

The survey also details the complicated arrangements for watering the meadows. At point C there was a 'trunk' (most likely an alternative word for 'conduit', but possibly a hollowed tree-trunk) laid under the river for draining Ratfyn meadows by a carriage on the south of Picket Meadows.

Hatches at point D were maintained by the neighbouring Earl's Farm to water the meadows on both sides of the river, and when shut down 'penned' water back to point E and thence across Ratfyn's meadows. Ratfyn paid Earl's Farm £5 for this service as without the hatches the meadows could

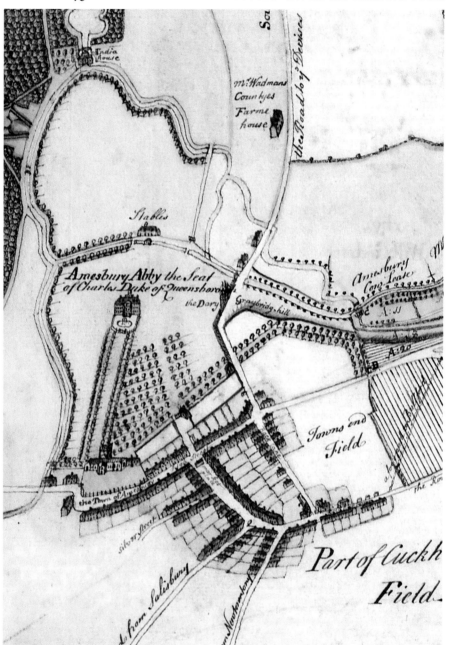

Detail of Godson's map, showing Amesbury town

Prospect from the 7 barrows east of Amberstbury to the opening of the Avenue of Stonehenge. &
A. the beginning of the avenue Stukeley Del.

William Stukeley's view of the Amesbury area from above Ratfyn Barrow, 1724

not be watered.[13] At point B stood an 'index' (finger post) pointing eastward and inscribed 'Ratfin Road begins here'.

The undated Ratfyn sketch,[14] a stray document in an estate collection largely concerned with places in north and west Wiltshire, may be roughly contemporary with Godson. Most names and much of the land use correspond, as well as the stated acreages of meadow and pasture. Crude and schematic, and now torn with a lacuna along the fold, its principal value is the bold representation of Ratfyn farmhouse and yard, enclosed by byres and sheds, which corroborates Godson's much smaller depiction. Equally bold on the sketch is another house, which is drawn beside the Bulford road; it is found also, albeit faintly drawn, on Godson's map, where it is labelled 'The Folly House'. It stood at what is still known as Folly Bottom, the modern road bridge over the A303 (and speed camera!) next to Solstice Park.

Godson's depiction of Amesbury town is greatly inferior to that of Flitcroft 22 years earlier, sending off the road to Newton Tony (now Smithfield Street and Earls Court Road) in the wrong direction, and omitting Tanners Lane, the loop in present Flower Lane which rejoins it to Salisbury Road. In mitigation the town's topography was of little interest to his clients, since Ratfyn owned no property there, and it is unclear why, except to locate Ratfyn in relation to it, he mapped the town at all. Some differences may reflect real changes between 1726 and 1748, notably cottages spreading southwards along the present Earl's Court Road, Smithfield Street and Salisbury Road. Flower Lane, which Flitcroft called by its usual name until the 20th century of Frog Lane, Godson described as Silver Street. His map thereby adds another, I think previously unrecorded, example of this common but intriguing West Country street name.[15] Also of interest are his depictions in perspective of Amesbury parish church, the abbey mansion and a substantial gatehouse at the end of Abbey Lane. The High Street is depicted as continuously built on both sides, the New Inn (now Comilla

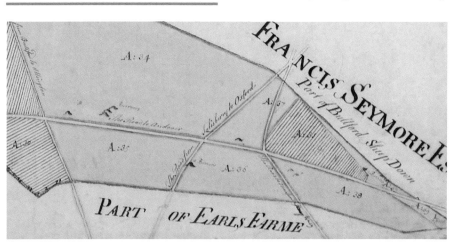

Detail of Godson's map, showing barrows on either side of the London road

House) conspicuous at its north-east end, and an archway shown leading into the George Inn courtyard. As many as 26 properties, perhaps the entire run of buildings on the north-west side of the High Street from the George to the New Inn, were to be devastated by fire three years after Godson drew them; the damage to their structures was estimated at £1,525 and to their contents £2,061.[16]

Within its obvious limits of scale and convention Godson's map appears to characterize Amesbury's streetscape as continuously lined with brick and tile houses, some with gables fronting the street, and noticeably larger, as would be expected, along Church Street, High Street and the Market Place (Salisbury Street) than around the edges of the built area. It serves to illustrate, therefore, an unusually detailed survey of manorial property in the town made a few years earlier, in 1741.[17] The document would be worthwhile publishing *in extenso*, but here examples must suffice (the spelling and punctuation have been modernised):

> Mrs Sarah Hays late Ratways: Five small tiled tenements in High street two story high in very bad repair, several parts of them being uncovered which greatly damages the building. The thing may be greatly improved if speedily undertaken. There is a handsome outlet but at present not occupied as gardens etc.

> Thos Towsey: The George Inn in High Street three story high tiled in tolerable repair, three six stall stables tiled in tolerable repair, three other large stables that are tiled on one side and thatched on the other. One of

the stables that is next to Mr Jones's is in very bad repair. A large thatched woodhouse in bad repair, an inward court and a large back court or barton. A paddock or close pasture some kitchen gardens etc with a cock pitt and kittle [skittle] alley.

Mr Richard Andrews, formerly Eatons: One tiled tenement in High Street three stories high skilling'd on the backside, a thatch'd workhouse all in tolerable repair, a small garden and close adjoining.

The final area of interest surrounds the depiction of archaeological features. Ratfyn Barrow has already been mentioned. A tree grows from it on Godson's plan, as it appears to also on the damaged Ratfyn sketch, but the tree is absent from Stukeley's view, taken in 1724, of the Amesbury area from a little further up the London road. This view, which shows a line of six smaller barrows running north-east from Ratfyn Barrow, parallels many of the topographical features present on Godson's map, including the open arable field in the foreground and the trees lining the river. It is disappointing that Godson did not depict these six barrows and thus corroborate Stukeley.[18] By way of compensation he did, however, include nine barrows on either side of the road to Andover (now the A303) as it climbs Beacon Hill. Of these, the group of three and a singleton in field A34 are probably a disc barrow and bell barrow excavated in 1956, and a triple bell barrow recorded nearby.[19] The bowl barrow near the eastern tip of the ploughed downland A31 survives (just) as a scheduled monument, very close to where the modern road from Bulford feeds into the A303.[20] But one of the two barrows in field A38 and those in A36 and A37 appear not to be on the current Historic Environment Register.

This short commentary on an interesting but neglected map merely highlights some points of particular interest to one observer. More generally it may serve to emphasise how much can be learned from early maps, and how rich is the vein of documentation about 18th-century Amesbury.[21]

Notes

1   WSA 944/1 (atlas); 944/2 (terrier).
2   E.g. for the town: *VCH Wilts*, 15, 20; *WANHM*, 102 (2009), 190; for the parish: *VCH Wilts*, 15, 41; Chandler, J and Goodhugh, P (2012) *Amesbury: history and description of a south Wiltshire town* (3rd ed), 20. The urban area is reproduced on the back cover of Crowley, D A *et al* (2003) *A history of Amesbury, Bulford and Durrington*.
3   H(ampshire) A(rchives), W/F 5/1.
4   In bundle WSA, 1953/68.
5   WSA 283/6, 1741 survey.

6 *VCH Wilts*, vol. 15, 29, 37; *VCH Hants*, vol. 2, 200-2.

7 HA, W/F 3/433/1-5; ibid, 76M70/T1-2. The provision of turkeys is clearly stated in the 1734 lease, and though the relevant portion of the document is damaged, seems to have been present on the same terms in 1720.

8 Ibid; *VCH Wilts*, vol. 15, 29; English Heritage, National Heritage List 1182605.

9 Assuming a standard perch of 16ft 6in.

10 Bendall, S (1997) *Dictionary of Land Surveyors and Local Mapmakers of Great Britain and Ireland, 1530-1850* (2nd ed), vol.2, 204. Estate maps by him of places in at least five counties survive in local record offices. I am grateful to John Hare and Tom Beaumont James for information about Godson's work.

11 Reproduced in James, T B (1997 ed) *Winchester*, 100.

12 Cobbett, W (1958 ed) *Rural Rides*, 309; cf *VCH Wilts*, vol. 15, 51.

13 I am grateful to Hadrian Cook, Gavin Bowie and Kathy Stearne for their comments on this arrangement.

14 WSA 1953/68. The collection includes also a little material relating to Normanton in the Woodford valley nearby.

15 Chandler, J (2009) *The Reflection in the Pond* , 130-1.

16 WSA 283/177; some affected properties can be located by reference to WSA 944/2, and WSA 283/6.

17 WSA 283/6, 1741 survey.

18 These barrows are discussed in Lawson, A (2007) *Chalkland: an archaeology of Stonehenge and its region*, 335-6.

19 *WANHM* 79 (1984), 39-91; Wiltshire Council Archaeology Service HER, SU14SE 671-3.

20 Ibid, SU14SE682.

21 I am most grateful to Hampshire County Council, Winchester City Council and Wiltshire Council for permission to reproduce and quote from documents in the care of Hampshire Archives and Wiltshire and Swindon Archives, and in particular for friendly assistance from David Rymill, Helen Taylor, Hadrian Cook and Steve Hobbs.

Some lost Salisbury street names

Sue Johnson

The publication of an article on the Belle Vue Estate, Salisbury,[1] which drew extensively on the building regulations records of the City Council (now kept at the Wiltshire and Swindon History Centre, reference WSA G23/760) prompted the completion of a project to input the summary data in a format allowing sorting by location or applicant name. The location listing produced a number of unfamiliar street names.

Checking the original records confirmed that, as expected, most were simple transcription errors, eg Rings, Allaway and Alexander for Kings, Albany and Queen Alexandra respectively. However four examples remained which could not be identified in any modern street index – Albert Road, Peters Road, Station Road and Church Street. The plans relating to Albert Road, off Victoria Road, were both for single houses, one for P Foot in 1933 and the other for S Clarke in 1936. This street name did exist briefly. It was approved at the General Purposes Committee meeting on 24 April 1929,[2] but shortly after the death of Bishop Donaldson it was renamed in his memory in 1936 following a suggestion from a Mr G T Pugh who lived in the road.[3] This followed the pattern of naming roads in the area after bishops of Salisbury, already established with Hamilton, Moberly, Wordsworth and Ridgeway.

Peters Road is listed as the location for a single plan, submitted by W Forder & Sons in 1934 for a number of houses. The road was to extend from Stratford Road to Castle Road and the application was for 91 bungalows. Initially approved on 1 October 1934 subject to alterations, it was subsequently rejected on 10 November that year. In 1935 the firm submitted amended plans for 109 houses but in the event these were never built, the land of the Old Sarum Building Estate being purchased by the City Council in order to retain an open space near Old Sarum. The purchase was partly financed by money left by Alderman J C Hudson, after whom Hudson's Field is named.[4]

Peters Road is not included in Peter Hart's work on the dates of Salisbury street names, compiled as a result of his searches though hundreds of city archives, suggesting that it was never officially agreed by the Council, but was presumably devised by the developers. It is referred to on another plan, for buildings to be erected on the Greyhound Racing Stadium, submitted in 1932, so had obviously been an accepted, if provisional, name for some time. It also existed in a physical sense in the form of a cinder track, referred to in the report of the conditions set by the executors of Alderman Hudson for making a grant for the acquisition of the land, where it is described as 'the proposed St. Peter's-road'.[5]

Station Road was the given location for Messrs Strong's application for alterations to the Railway Hotel in 1924. It is now known as South Western Road, a name which had existed since at least the 1871 census.[6] Hart gives no date for the official naming of this road, but states that it was called Station Road in an 1891 directory.[7] Possibly Station Road was the term used by locals, who knew they meant the street by the Fisherton railway station, not the one at Milford, whereas officaldom needed a more definite name.

A further application relating to the Railway Hotel in 1925 gives its location as Church Street (the building is on a corner). This name is also used in two plans relating to Hulse House (1917 and 1924). A 1919 submission relating to Carlton House makes the location clear – Church Street, Fisherton. In 1937 and 1938 two plans refer to Fisherton Church Street. This was the format normally used to distinguish this Church Street from the two others which existed in the city, in St Edmund's and St Martin's parishes. Both now have their parish designation incorporated as the first element of their names, but Fisherton Church Street did not follow that route. Instead it was renamed in the mid 20th century as an extension to Mill Road, the title also adopted for the stretch of road formerly called Harcourt Bridge Road, so that today the name applies to the whole length of the thoroughfare from Crane Bridge Road to Great Western Road.

References

Garland, K, 2010, *A Short History of Greyhound Racing in Salisbury*, South Wiltshire Industrial Archaeology Society, Historical Monograph 20
Hart, P, 2003, *Salisbury and Wilton Street Names*, privately published
Kelly's Directory of Salisbury, 1947

At the Wiltshire and Swindon History Centre

Meeting hall, Hulse House, Church Street, Lady Hulse, G23/760/153, 1917
Additions to house, 1 Carlton House, Church Street, Fisherton, Miss Douglas, G23/760/179, 1919

Alterations, Railway Hotel, Station Road, Strong & Co, G23/760/268, 1924
Alterations to Hulse House, 6 Church Street, Miss W Young, G23/760/285, 1924
Extensions, Railway Hotel, Church Street, Strong & Co. G23/760/321, 1925
Buildings on Greyhound Racing Stadium, Castle Road, G23/760/712, 1932
House, Albert Road, P Foot, G23/760/767, 1933
Houses, Peters Road, W Forder & Sons, G23/760/893, 1934 [folder includes the 1935 plan]
House, Albert Road, S Clarke, G23/760/1046, 1936
House, Fisherton Church Street, F Lucas, G23/760/1172, 1937
Two houses, Fisherton Church Street, F Lucas, G23/760/1221, 1938

Notes

1 Minting, Andrew (2012) 'The Belle Vue Estate, an early 20th century suburb'. *Sarum Chronicle* 12, 65–80
2 Hart, 27
3 *Salisbury Times* 7 February 1936, 4, City Council Report
4 Hart, 30; *Salisbury Times* 8 February 1935 February, 4, bequest of JCH; 9, submission of plans by Forder
5 *Salisbury Journal* 10 January 1936, 9, City Council Report
6 TNA RG 10/1951, ff 69–70
7 Hart, 15

The Sculptor, Sir Alfred Gilbert RA (1854–1934): Wiltshire Connections

David Richards

The visitor to the charming, Saxon market town of Wilton, approaching from Salisbury, will follow the great brick wall that encloses the home park of Wilton House. Near the imposing triumphal arch, that frames the mansion's gilded iron entrance gates, is a bronze statue of a man prominently positioned on a stone plinth, at the side of the busy A30 road.

It depicts George Robert Charles Herbert, the 13th Earl of Pembroke (1850-1895) dressed in the uniform of a Colonel of the 1st Wiltshire Rifle Volunteers. Dogged by ill health as a young man, a visit to the South Pacific in a private yacht was proposed. On arrival in Tahiti he was entranced by the islands and their people. He was even tempted to marry 'a wonderfully pretty young girl' but the prospect of the disapproval of his 'over-fastidious relations' in Wilton made him change his mind. On leaving, he was shipwrecked on a desert island and ultimately rescued by a Scandinavian schooner called the *Duke of Edinburgh*.[1] Back in England he married Lady Gertrude Talbot, daughter of the Earl of Shrewsbury and was appointed Under Secretary for War. Sadly he died at the early age of 45 suffering from tuberculosis.[2]

A committee was set up in Wilton to organize the creation of a memorial to him. Gertrude, his widow, chose the popular and distinguished artist Alfred Gilbert to sculpt a life size bronze statue. Gilbert was born in London, the son of an organist, also named Alfred Gilbert (1828-65), who himself had been born in Salisbury and baptized in the parish church of St Thomas. Alfred senior's father, Francis Gilbert (1782-1850) was the

Roadside statue of the 13th Earl of Pembroke near entrance to Wilton House. Photograph by author.

owner of a foundry and an ironmongery business, trading in Silver Street in Salisbury.[3] The business prospered and at the time of the wedding of his eldest son, Alfred Snr, he is describing himself in the census as a 'gentleman' employing nine men.[4] It was hoped Alfred Jnr would study medicine but he failed the examinations. Instead he began a lengthy period of study in this country, Paris and Rome to become a sculptor.

His development of a personal, distinctive style quickly brought him success. When the upper echelons of society began offering commissions, he was deluged with work. Unfortunately, he could never say no and many works took years and years to complete. His debts increased, he fell out with the Royal family, lived in Bruges in self imposed exile and was ultimately stripped of his position as a Royal Academician. In 1926 King George V invited him to return to England to complete the tomb of the Duke of Clarence at Windsor. In 1932 he was re-elected RA and knighted. The Pembroke statue took over five years to complete despite Lady Pembroke's repeated questioning visits to Gilbert's studio.[5] It was not greeted with unalloyed approval. The local paper suggested that the head was too small, the shoulders were too broad and the face untrue. On May 19, 1900, the Leader of the House of Commons, Arthur Balfour, unveiled the statue against a background of loyal cheering and applause from a 4000 strong crowd. Afterwards in replying to the vote of thanks, Balfour felt obliged to rejoice in the recent relief of Mafeking. Here, in the provincial backwater of the little town of Wilton, a work of fine art by a significant national artist representing a much loved aristocrat was unveiled by a world class statesman and reported nationally by *The Times* of London.[6]

In 1887 a memorial by Gilbert in Westminster Abbey, was dedicated to a local Salisbury man, Henry Fawcett (1833-84), former MP and Post Master General.[7] The turquoise and garnets which had adorned the memorial disappeared at the time of the 1902 coronation.

In 1892, Gilbert created an exquisite monument in St Katherine's Church, Savernake near Marlborough, to a daughter of the 11th Earl of Pembroke, Mary Caroline Herbert, Marchioness of Ailesbury, showing her as an extraordinary gilded white figure clasping, and standing behind, a stylized metal tree.

Gilbert's extraordinary, tall, Art Nouveau work of 1887 is both a font and a memorial to John Boteville Thynne (1868–1887) the youngest son of the 4th Marquess of Bath, in the Bath Chapel of the Church of St Peter and St Paul, Longbridge Deverill. Its style was later compared to Gaudi by Nicholas Pevsner. Pevsner described this and the Ailesbury work as 'fabulous monuments' and the only ones from the latter half of the 19th century, in Wiltshire, that were worthy of attention.[8]

Gilbert's 1887 Art Nouveau design for the Mayor of Preston's chain of office provoked a nationwide interest in his skill as a goldsmith. When the present Salisbury mayoral chain was being commissioned in 1893, Gilbert's advice was sought and given to the Birmingham jeweler, JW Tonks, who made it.[9]

Gilbert's most famous work Eros, in London's Piccadilly, was the world's first cast aluminium statue. Perhaps it is not too much to believe that Gilbert's passion for fine art metal work had its roots in his Salisbury grandfather's craft of iron founding.

One hundred years on, Gilbert's public art in Wilton has achieved the status of a Grade II listed monument. Time may have obscured some of the detail of its story but that striking image, towering nine feet over passers-by, remains a potent element in the modern town's understanding of its historical identity.

Notes

1   Lever, Tresham, 1967, *The Herberts of Wilton,* John Murray, 228-9
2   *Oxford Dictionary of National Biography,* 2014
3   *Pigot's Trade Directory 1844.* Francis Gilbert is described as an ironmonger and iron founder
4   Dorment, Richard, 1985, *Alfred Gilbert,* Yale University Press, 4
5   Ibid. 179
6   *The Times* (London, England), Monday, May 21, 1900, 15
7   *The Times* (London, England), January 29, 1887
8   Pevsner, Nicholas and Cherry, Bridget 1975, *The Buildings of England. Wiltshire,* Penguin Books, 55
9   Haskins, Charles, 1910, *The Salisbury Corporation Pictures and Plate,* Bennett Brothers, 211

An 18th century tourist's view of South Wiltshire

Sue Johnson

On 4 August 1798 Thomas R Hall left London in the company of Captain W Trevanion of the Derby Regiment of Militia at the start of a lengthy tour of southern England. His account of the journey, now at the Wiltshire and Swindon History Centre,[1] tells how they headed first for Brighton then worked their way along the coast to Exeter. The return journey also followed the coast to begin with, including a trip to Guernsey and Jersey, but then turned inland to include visits to various south Wiltshire places. Leaving Blandford on 19 September they took the road to Shaftesbury and Hindon.

> Shaftesbury stands high & commands an excellent view, we dined there & in our road forward had a distant glimpse of Wardour Castle, the antient residence of the Catholic Earls of Arundel. We heard that it was well worth seeing, but were too late in the day. Slept at Hindon, which is a borough Town, but something like an Irish one.
>
> Thurs Sep 20th. Set off early to see Font-hill belonging to Mr. Beckford. [at foot of page is note 'Taken down after the abbey was built'] The approach to the house,[2] under an elegant arched porters lodge, & by the side of an extensive piece of water, well skirted with wood, is handsome; but the road, I think, too straight.
>
> The house appears large, built of clean stone from the estate, & has two spacious wings. The furniture, we understood, was the most expensive in England. Every chair is gilt & silk curtains in most of the rooms, everything in short finished & furnished in the most sumptuous style.
>
> The Entrance Hall is lofty & noble – the other apartments on as

good a scale, but not upon the largest. The house seems a good one to live in, but as a place of modern Architecture, by no means equal to Keddlestone.[3]

The pictures seem fine & valuable, among them is the original set of Hogarth's Rakes Progress. One of the Rooms down stairs, is filled up in a singular manner resembling a Turkish Tent, & has a beautiful appearance.

A large building in the Park, which they call the Abbey, is nearly finished at an immense expence, but no one is yet permitted to see it. [note at foot of page: N.B. 1826 – This abbey has been dismantled & its loft tower fallen down.']

Twelve good miles conveyed us from the <u>perishable magnificence</u> of the present age, to the venerable walls, & time-defying ornaments & antiquities, Roman and Greecian, of Wilton Abbey. The contrast excessive. Nothing at Font-hill in existence fifty years ago; nothing scarcely at Wilton less than five, or fifteen-hundred years old. The original busts & statues, are more numerous here perhaps than at any other house in England. A conniseur in Antiques must find many weeks amusement in the collection. In a gallery over the great hall are many suits of armour, taken by one of the Earls of Pembroke, at St Quintin.

In the hunting Room the Pannels are painted to represent 18 different sports, some of them well done & others very whimsical. At Font-hill the Rooms are distinguished by the variety, or richness of their furniture, which after the first, is tiresome, & by its sameness ceases to attract notice – at Wilton every Apartment presents us with some classic acquaintance, whose features & physiognomy, faithfully preserved teach us to connect, or call to mind the fancied likeness, which the perusal of their actions may have suggested in their imaginations.

The town of Wilton has been of great consequence, & is still the County Town, (tho' publick business is transacted at Salisbury), now famous for its carpets.

Only 3 miles from New Sarum, where we arrived at four, & put up at the Antelope. Salisbury being a famous place for Cutlery, bought some razors there.

Friday 21st. Walked to the Cathedral, the inside of which has lately been cleaned & put in order & is now one of the most complete & spacious in England.

The King gave them their Organ, & the painted glass came from Birmingham.

The spire said to be the highest in the country. Turned again out of the Great Road to Amesbury, to see Stonehenge, two miles distant from it. In our way passed Old Sarum, which has the appearance of a Roman Camp, with a wide interval between its inward & outward Ditch not a single house on it; & only one alehouse, standing alone, at all near it.

A large old manor house stands out of Amesbury, which is rented by a numerous society of Nuns;[4] some of whom, the Turnpike woman said, it was a vast pity should be there.

The situation, for the purpose, could hardly be surpassed, I should think, by any they fled from; having plenty of wood & water on the domain & a quiet, retired market Town adjoining. The Abbey belongs to Old Q (Duke of Queensbury) & what is wonderful, he never comes to visit it.[5]

The visit to Amesbury concluded the Wiltshire section of the trip, the travellers continuing their journey to London via Andover, Whitchurch and Reading and finally reaching their destination on 24 September. However Mr Hall was obviously impressed by Stonehenge – at the foot of the page he added:

P.S. Forgot to mention that Stonehenge fully answered our expectations, certainly the most curious antique in the kingdom.

Notes

1 WSA 776/652 Diary of Thomas R Hall recording his tour on horseback and by coach, in the company of Captain W Trevanion, 1798. The original has dashes to indicate the end of sentences, full stops are used in this transcript for convenience.
2 This is a description of the house known as 'Fonthill Splendens', built c 1755 and mostly demolished by 1807.
3 He presumably means Kedleston Hall, Derbyshire, a fine 18th century house by Robert Adam.
4 Amesbury Abbey was occupied 1794–1800 by refugee nuns from Louvain.
5 William Douglas, 4th Duke of Queensberry, was absentee owner from 1778 until his death in 1820.

Diary extract by kind permission of Wiltshire and Swindon Archives.

'Please come to Odstock and watch the peewits on the downs'[1]: Edward Brian Seago (1910–74) and Salisbury

John Elliott

Ted Seago's gifts will long be remembered, valued and loved. His work was in the best tradition of that particularly English school of landscape artists with which few others can compare.
HRH The Prince of Wales[2]

The association between John Constable and Salisbury is well recognized; that between Edward Seago and the Salisbury area is little known, yet, as we will see, he lived at Old Sarum and Britford during the 1939-45 war and was based at Wilton House. Seago is now considered to be one of the 'great' British landscape painters and his time in Wiltshire saw the production of some of his finest work. His paintings are highly collectable and attract premium prices whenever they become available.

Edward Seago was born into a middle-class Norwich family being the youngest of two boys. His father was the area manager for a large firm of coal merchants and the family lived in a three-storey, semi-detached house in Christchurch Road, Norwich. Seago suffered from a heart condition which limited his education and during the long hours of resting he became an avid drawer and painter, though his parents showed little interest in what was to become his passion.

In 1923 he became associated with the already established artist, Bertram Priestman, and was taught by him before becoming involved with a circus. The circus life, and the bright colours they used, attracted Seago. They

Water Meadow near Salisbury Oil on board. 12"x9.5". The view is from Britford and shows the Poplar trees that Seago mentions specifically. Image © The Estate of Edward Seago, courtesy of Portland Gallery, London

offered adventure and a touch of the exotic. He toured England, Ireland and France with them, recording much of his experiences in *Circus Company* (1933), *Sons of Sawdust* (1934) and *Caravan* (1937).[3] He also painted scenes to accompany books of poetry by John Masefield.[4]

Seago suffered from a heart problem (paroxysmal tachycardia) which should have excluded him from military service, though by a mixture of determination and economy with the truth he managed to get enrolled as a war artist. However, he continued to lobby for a more active role and eventually trained in camouflage at the School of Military Engineers at Chatham and served as a camouflage officer within the Royal Engineers.

For part of the war he was stationed at Wilton House, lived near Salisbury and was given the rank of Major as the Camouflage Officer for the 5th Corp, Southern Command. Initially he lived at the School of Army Co-operation at Old Sarum RAF station. According to Seago's biographer, this was 'a cheerful little station which boasted a comfortable, old-fashioned type of mess shared by both Army and RAF officers and retained its peacetime practice of being staffed by civilian batmen'.[5] Seago also enjoyed working at Wilton House, and particularly liked 'the daffodils gilding the lawns under the great cedars and warming, in their reflection, the austerity of the pale stone of the one-time abbey'.[6]

The General Officer Commander-in-Chief of Southern Command was Claude Auchinleck, with whom Seago soon developed a friendly relationship, and the two men spent time painting together. Much the same happened later when Lieutenant General Sir Harold Alexander (later Field Marshal Earl Alexander of Tunis) replaced Auchinleck.

While at Old Sarum Seago continued something he had started in his youth - studying the sky in detail – the cirrus, nimbus and cumulus clouds and the air currents that affected them. He became eager to fly so that he could 'see the other side of the clouds' and inspect them more closely.[7] A colleague started giving him lessons in a dual-control Miles Magister and he went solo after twelve hours instruction, recording how:

> There was only one thing that mattered: I was alone in the sky. A new life had begun. The blue sky had become an ocean to voyage upon. The clouds, countries to explore.[8]

From then on his name appeared in the flight log two or three times every week.

Life at Old Sarum may have been better than that provided in many airfields but Seago wanted something more permanent. He found it in Britford, where he rented the cottage that was in the grounds of the 5th Corp Officers' Mess. The cottage Seago used is now known as Moat Cottage and the Officers' Mess was located in the large detached house (currently known as Moat House) which is now divided into two dwellings. Moat House originated in the seventeenth century with substantial remodelling and additions in 1766 and the early nineteenth century. It is in the Gothick style. The house was the property of the Jervoise family from 1542. Richard Jervoise added the north wing and vaulted ground floor wine cellar c1740. In 1766 Tristram Jervoise added a brick front facade with battlement bays and Gothick detail, and around 1820 George Jervoise added a south range and encased the sides in matching yellow brick. The large moat surrounding the house may be an 18th century remodelling of an earlier one.

Moat Cottage, where Seago lived, is still there, though somewhat extended, but in the 1940s it was a simple two-up, two-down cottage with a walled garden.[9] It was located in a rural setting close to the river Avon and was surrounded on three sides by a moat that was fed by the river.[10] It was

cold and damp, especially in the winter, initially had no electricity and all the water had to be pumped by hand, but it was home. The rent was £20 a year. Roses dominated the garden and 'In the distance, the spire of Salisbury Cathedral rose like a finger'.[11] Seago recorded how:

> In my cottage in Wiltshire the river winds through the water meadows within a hundred yards of my door. Tall reeds and clumps of purple loosestrife shield the sluice gates in the river bank, and the crowsfoot flower spatters the clear water. From my window I can see the spire of Salisbury Cathedral rising against the sky above the fringe of poplar trees,[12] and on autumn evenings the mist spreads itself across the marsh. I have walked the surrounding country of my cottage at all times of day in every season of the year. I have known the delight of finding an endless quantity of subjects within a stone's throw of my gate. I have taken my paints at a moment's notice to make a brief note of a passing mood, and, even more important, I have watched my subjects in all weathers, until, to quote an old waterman, "I know the name of every blade of grass".[13]

The Haunch of Venison in central Salisbury was also a favourite as it provided hot baths and a good dinner. The painter Augustus John (1878-1961) also drank there. Seago's party trick was to flick a coin with a postage stamp attached so that the stamp stuck on the ceiling.

The time at Britford was one of the really happy phases in Seago's life. He loved the countryside and especially the view of Salisbury Cathedral that he had from his cottage – 'the most beautiful spire in England'.[14] Later, when living in Norfolk, he dreamt about the Britford cottage and what it was then like. Especially important to him was the view:

> from the hatchery half a mile down the river from Harnham Bridge. From there one looks back at the spire and its reflection in the still water beneath. From there, also, one can watch the sun go down behind the Cathedral; I have often stayed until the spire becomes an inky silhouette, and the last amber light fades from the river.[15]

While he did occasionally paint portraits, Seago is best known for his landscapes and for the rather unique way he depicts the English countryside. There are often long views with the colours and the arrangement of hills

Opposite: *The East Window* (1944) Oil on board. 19"x15". This is a depiction of the inside of Moat Cottage and shows Vernon Russell Smith illuminated by the morning light which is coming through the window. Seago used poetic license with the painting which is actually of a west window and the light is from the afternoon sun. Image © The Estate of Edward Seago, courtesy of Portland Gallery, London

The White Kitchen (*c*.1942–3) Oil on canvas. 30"x25". Here Seago depicts a simple scene from within Moat Cottage: the kitchen complete with leeks, onions, tomatoes and the washing! Image © The Estate of Edward Seago, courtesy of Portland Gallery, London

and fields being used to create aerial perspective. Water is also often a feature, many paintings being based on river banks with the water being used to reflect the landscape. The effect of light and shade are strong features in his work. The contrast of verticals and horizontals were used to add interest, and he would have been particularly attracted to the way Salisbury Cathedral thrusts vertically from a rather flat valley landscape and how this verticality is mirrored by the poplar trees that lay between it and Britford. He recounted how:

> I wonder who had the happy idea of planting the poplars by the river at Salisbury? I believe they are about fifty years old – so Constable did not know them. Maybe it was he who first suggested them, for I'm sure he would have loved to see them when he walked in those quiet meadows. I have watched them so often from my cottage window, with the cathedral spire rising behind them. There have been glorious moments when the spire has been caught by sunlight and the trees darkened by shadow, and they have looked more than ever as sentinals standing guard. In a way they are sentinals for their wood is difficult to burn, and a belt of them will check a forest fire.[16]

The area offered numerous painting opportunities. He regularly recollected how he set out for the day and walked on the downs on either side of the Avon, sketching, painting and just enjoying the countryside. He also used the landscape close to the Britford cottage and described how:

> I like to take my paints and make several hurried colour notes. I have collected scores of these brush–jottings, and each time I do one I learn something I never knew before. I have done several of them in one morning, sitting in the meadow by my cottage. There is no need to move from one place to another, for there are beautiful subjects which–ever way I look. In one direction there is the tall black poplar which grows within a few feet of the river, and beyond it are the water meadows and the spire of Salisbury Cathedral. If I look the other way I see the bend in the river and Poulter's farm, and the low bridge where the cattle loiter when they come of their own accord from the meadows at milking time. But very often I paint the same subject many times, with the sunlight catching a different part of the landscape. Within the space of a few minutes I have seen the cathedral spire turn from a shell-pink ghost to a blue-grey silhouette. The line of poplar trees in front of it change in the reverse order; when the spire is brightly lit the trees are very dark, and when the spire is swept by shadow the trees glitter with silver light.[17]

Seago painted many pictures of the Salisbury area, including one where two nuns stand silhouetted against the cathedral that is in the background.

Two Nuns 20 x 16 ins. Oil on canvas. Painted from a hill overlooking Salisbury with the cathedral very visible. Image courtesy of Sotheby's

It was most probably painted from the ridge above Standlynch and between it and Pepperbox Hill and is most likely a depiction of two of the Sisters of Mercy from St Elizabeth Convent in Exeter Street who were active in Salisbury until late in the 1900s.[18] He wrote:

> Sometimes, on my walks near Salisbury, I have passed two nuns stepping briskly along the country lanes – the wind billows their full blue robes and flutters the white wings of their headdress. Normally they walk in pairs, but sometimes I see one of them with a number of small children. The children are dressed alike in pinafores or tunics of gay colours. They walk happily in groups, or in couples holding hands. They appear to be of about the same age, perhaps six or seven years old, and they look such jolly kids, with their hair tousled by the wind and their young faces as fresh as the breezy day.[19]

So strong was the affection for southern Wiltshire that Seago took exception to the railway advertisements which encouraged people to visit various seaside resorts, and instead suggested that the adverts should say: 'Please come to Odstock and watch the peewits on the downs.'[20] He also wrote:

> I should like to think that, when I die this body of mine will be turned to ashes and cast to the winds from a high green hill. I suppose it wouldn't matter in which part of the world the hill might happen to be; but, if I could make my choice, I think it would be a grassy slope in Wiltshire. A strong gentle slope which stoops to cradle a clear river winding through the dear green Wiltshire meadows.[21]

Seago designed the insignia for the airborne forces and became a war artist in mainland Europe. He wrote *Peace in War* (1943), *High Endeavour* (1944) and *With the Allied Armies in Italy* (1945).[22]

After the war he settled in Norfolk and lived for many years at the Dutch House in Ludham. He used his own boat as a mobile studio to explore and paint both Norfolk and the near continent. He travelled widely and exhibited in Canada, South Africa and the United States and was elected to the Royal Society of British Artists in 1946, made an associate of the Royal Society of Watercolour Painters in 1957 and became a full member two years later.

Seago was a special favourite of the Royal family and extensive numbers of his paintings have been collected by The Queen Mother, The Duke of Edinburgh and Prince Charles. He was one of the artists who were invited to paint the 1952 coronation and for 21 years stayed at Sandringham each

Early Morning, Britford Lane 1942, Oil on canvas. 202"x24". Image © The Estate of Edward Seago, courtesy of Portland Gallery, London

January and July when he painted with the Duke of Edinburgh. He painted portraits of George VI, the Queen Mother, Queen Elizabeth II, Prince Philip and Princess Margaret. In 1956-7 he accompanied the Duke of Edinburgh on the royal yacht as it toured Antarctica. Prince Charles fondly remembers the 'almost annual January visits with my father to the Dutch House at Ludham' and how he was surrounded by Seago's paintings at home. He became fascinated and 'In the end I wrote to the expert himself and asked if I could come over to visit him from Sandringham and pick up a few useful hints'.[23] A tutorial followed and 'It was one of the most impressive demonstrations of sheer creativity I have ever seen … I went away inspired'.[24]

Regular exhibitions followed plus visits to Hong Kong, Burma, Thailand, South Africa, Greece, Morocco and Turkey. Edward Seago died in London during 1974 of a brain tumour after having been taken ill while staying at his holiday home in Sardinia.[25] His ashes were scattered in Norfolk.

Notes

1   Edward Seago, 1947, *A Canvas to Cover*, Collins 18 & 24
2   Foreword to Jean Goodman, 1978, *Edward Seago: The Other Side of the Canvas,*, William Collins, 12
3   The first two were published by Putnam of London and *Caravan* was published by Collins.
4   *The Country Scene* (1937), *Tribute to Ballet* (1938) and *A Generation Risen* (1942).
5   Jean Goodman, 1978, 155
6   Ibid, 151
7   Ibid, 157
8   Ibid, 157
9   Hugh and Peggy Shortt lived there later when Hugh was the curator of the Salisbury & South Wiltshire Museum.
10 The river feeds a carrier which then feeds the moat. The principal purpose of the carrier was to feed the water meadows.
11 Ibid, 164
12 The poplars still exist and are located along one bank of the river.
13 Edward Seago,1947, 81
14 Ibid, 91
15 Ibid, 91
16 Ibid, 53
17 Ibid, 117
18 I am grateful to Jane Howells for identifying the nuns. St Elizabeth House is still there but is now subdivided between Elizabeth House Social Centre, accommodation for Alabare clients and a hall for St Osmund's church.
19 Edward Seago, 1947, 91
20 Ibid, 18 & 24
21 Ibid, 100. Peter Seymour subsequently scattered his ashes over the Norfolk marshes where he had lived for a major part of his life.
22 All published by Collins.
23 Ibid, 11-12
24 Ibid, 236
25 Seago had a holiday home in Sardinia: Sa Conca at Porto Cervo. See http://www.akvillas.com/luxury-villas-italy/luxury-villas-sardinia/sa-conca.cfm   [accessed January 2014].

John Jabez Edwin Mayall, Interior of the North Transept of the Crystal Palace, 1851. Daguerreotype. Digital image courtesy of The J Paul Getty Museum.

Salisbury & District and the Great Exhibition

Anthony Hamber and Jane Howells

While exhibitions had become part of mid-19th century popular culture, nothing on a local, regional or national level had taken place that was comparable to the 1851 Great Exhibition of the Works of Industry of All Nations.

On the 17 October 1849 Prince Albert and Henry Cole, who became the first Director of what is today the Victoria and Albert Museum, made speeches at the Mansion House in London outlining the plans for the 'Great Exhibition'. This initiative was in part due to impetus built up by the *Exposition Nationale des Produits de l'Agriculture et de l'Industrie* held in Paris earlier that year. Knowledge of this exhibition was known to Salisbury inhabitants through both national and local newspapers of the time.[1]

How the population of Salisbury reacted to and embraced the Great Exhibition can be viewed and analysed through the contemporary local press; primarily the *Salisbury & Winchester Journal* (*SJ*) and, as a counterpoint, the *Salisbury & Wiltshire Herald* (*SWH*).[2]

Salisbury was seen by the Exhibition's organisers as part of the provincial infrastructure supporting the venture. Although commissioners were appointed 'to promote and publicize the exhibition in every town'[3] it was not feasible that they should go everywhere, and Salisbury does appear to have been targeted. Herbert Byng Hall (1805-1883) was appointed by the Royal Commissioners to 'promote the interests of the Exhibition of 1851' in the West Country. Hall later recounted his visit to Salisbury which took place on 1 May 1850. 'In the performance of those duties, I held public meetings, formed local committees, and selected local honorary secretaries.' He was not optimistic about the outcome.

Visit with me a few towns in the county of Wiltshire—for instance, Salisbury—a loyal city, whose chief magistrate had dined with his hospitable official brother in the great metropolis and there beheld the consort of his sovereign and heard the noble sentiments which fell from his lips.

On the subject of the Great Exhibition being named to him, he at once called a public meeting of his townsmen and the neighbourhood, and as chairman energetically aided in passing resolutions in approval of the vast undertaking. A committee was also formed, and slight subscriptions raised. Enthusiasm, however, on the subject, there was little or none; in fact, nine-tenths of the persons who gathered there doubtless came as a mere matter of curiosity, as would they have attended any other meeting having reference to any other object—good, bad, or indifferent.[4]

Byng was keen to underline two features of the Exhibition; the universality of the undertaking, and the absence of any party or political feeling and 'expressed the hope that that Salisbury and Wilton would exhibit their productions at the Exhibition...'.[5] However, analysis by Auerbach has indicated significant political divides between those towns and cities that supported, or did not support, the Exhibition.[6]

The mayor did indeed go to promotional banquets attended by Prince Albert, at York[7] and at the Mansion House in London where the Lord Mayor of London had invited the 'chief municipal authorities of nearly all England'.[8] The official council line throughout was to support the project, 'one of the greatest and noblest ever brought before a British public'[9] if in a somewhat cautious way.

Opinions amongst the citizens of Salisbury were divided. Some were sceptical: it was noted in February 1851 that

A few persons have clubbed together in this city, to subscribe funds for a trip to the "World's Fair" next summer; and they held a meeting at a small inn, on Tuesday evening last, to form their regulations: but the general feeling here is not at all favourable to this "monster" project for draining off the summer trade of the provinces into London.[10]

Others were more positive. 'I think Salisbury will benefit from it' was a view expressed in May 1850. Coard W Squarey, a local solicitor of Rollestone Street who would be mayor of Salisbury 1857-58, and Captain Giles Emly of The Close, a retired member of the East India Company Artillery, were in agreement that as a result of such an exhibition '... everything we make use of, whether as regards articles of clothing, or the preparation of our food' would be improved. Visitors would come to London to the Exhibition and then visit attractions elsewhere that would include Stonehenge, the

Cathedral, and Old Sarum.[11] By the middle of the 19th century the tourist trade was already of significance to Salisbury's economy generating demand for transport, accommodation and refreshments. Nationally, a potential increase in tourism was used by the Royal Commissioners to encourage involvement in the exhibition in the provinces.[12]

Some, such as William James Chaplin (1787-1859), had a vested interest to promote the exhibition. Chaplin was an influential and well-connected businessman,[13] who was Liberal MP for Salisbury between 1847 and 1857. To a significant extent he owed his election to his chairmanship of the London & South Western Railway (LSWR), which, it was considered, would give him power to confer business benefits upon the city.[14] These expectations were fulfilled to a degree when the contract for new trucks and wagons for the Salisbury and Bishopstoke railway was given to a Salisbury iron-founder, Thomas Wolferson. Chaplin had a direct interest in promoting LSWR trains to carry visitors to the Great Exhibition from Salisbury.

After receiving the national communication from Her Majesty's Commissioners for the Exhibition of the Works of Industry of All Nations to be held in the year 1851, the council took a little time, but then '... unanimously resolved that a Committee be appointed ... for the purpose of raising subscriptions and of promoting the success of the intended Exhibition ...'.[15]

So the local committee of councillors and 'other inhabitants of the city' was formed, chaired by the mayor. In 1849-50 this was Dr Thomas Richard Moore (b1815), a Physician and General Practitioner who lived in Endless Street. He was succeeded in November 1850 by George Brown, a bookseller and stationer, newsagent and vendor of patent medicines in the New Canal.[16] These two men headed the organisation of the local response and involvement with the exhibition, ably assisted by the secretary.

Charles L Lee, a local solicitor was the Secretary and Treasurer. He would be retiring, after 30 years public service as assistant Town Clerk, in July 1851 at the height of the Exhibition. He was presented with a scroll on vellum in recognition of his 'assiduous and strict attention to the duties entrusted to him'.[17] His administrative skills were put to good use by the Exhibition local committee.

Towards the end of April 1850 a major event was advertised: 'Merchants, Bankers, and Traders of this City and Vicinity are invited to attend [a public meeting] to consider and adopt measures for promoting the success and accomplishing the Object of the proposed Exhibition of the Works of Industry of All Nations.'[18] So seeds were being sown, and apparently specific interests in the city were being targeted.

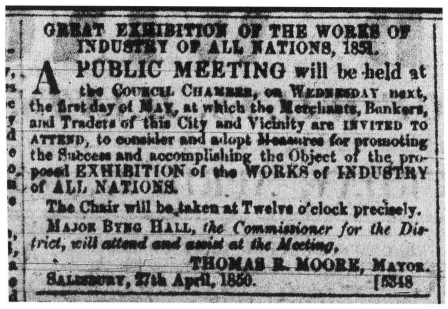

GREAT EXHIBITION OF THE WORKS OF INDUSTRY OF ALL NATIONS, 1851.

A PUBLIC MEETING will be held at the Council Chamber, on Wednesday next, the first day of May, at which the Merchants, Bankers, and Traders of this City and Vicinity are INVITED TO ATTEND, to consider and adopt Measures for promoting the Success and accomplishing the Object of the proposed EXHIBITION of the WORKS of INDUSTRY of ALL NATIONS.

The Chair will be taken at Twelve o'clock precisely.

MAJOR BYNG HALL, the Commissioner for the District, will attend and assist at the Meeting,

THOMAS B. MOORE, Mayor.

Salisbury, 27th April, 1850.   [5848

Salisbury Journal, Saturday 26th April 1850

This was the meeting on the 1 May 1850 held at the Council Chamber attended by the visiting Major Herbert Byng Hall, quoted above. A lengthy report of the meeting was published, including the contribution from Hall who commented that '[t]he attendance, though not numerous, was highly respectable'. Colonel Buckley of New Hall, one of Salisbury's MPs from 1853, 'thought the small attendance was due to the object not being understood' and Reverend Newton Smart, Vicar of Alderbury, considered it 'most unfortunate that the impression should have gone abroad that it was anything to do with Free Trade.'[19]

What might have been considered appropriate contributions from the area for exhibition? Mr W. Smith, who seconded the resolution approving local involvement in the Exhibition, stated that 'as *Salisbury has no manufacturers* [our italics]… circulars should be sent round to the churchwardens and ministers of the various parishes within 15 miles of the city to induce them to collect subscriptions in aid of the undertaking.....'.[20] Smith was not strictly accurate. Salisbury did have a long-established, but declining and increasingly specialised industry in cutlery manufacture. And although the local economy had altered from the dominance of woollen textiles of earlier centuries, there were varied enterprises that produced inputs for commercial agriculture, and those which used agricultural raw materials. These included malthouses and breweries, leatherworks, horsehair cloth manufacture, whips, baskets and brushes. However Salisbury was also evolving into a service centre for the surrounding area; the products of lawyers, bankers, schools, hotels, and retail outlets were perhaps less conducive to display in an international exhibition.

Subscription lists were published, and these included all the great and good of the city. The obligation for the Salisbury Local Committee to raise funds through subscriptions for the Commissioners in London continued through 1850 into the following year. Some insights into the funding structure were mentioned in the *SJ* in August 1850 and more contributions were listed, together with the statement 'subscription books continue open at the several banks and with the Hon Sec Mr Lee.'[21] In the event, the Local Committee was able to raise some £80 16s from local subscriptions. After deductions for local expenses £70 19s was paid to the Royal Commissioners.

The *SJ* appreciated that the cost of entry to the Great Exhibition might be prohibitive and hoped that subscriptions might be used to 'regulate the amount to be paid for entrance that all classes may have access to the Exhibition.'[22] Reports of the amounts sent in by various Local Committees 'within the sphere of our circulation' perhaps represented an element of competition between communities, and could be interpreted as a measure of the differing support for the project. When Salisbury had contributed £62 3s 0d, Devizes offered £14 0s 0d, and Poole £20 10s 0d; but Bridport had sent £69 19s 0d, Yeovil £70 15s 0d and Bath £146 14s 6d.[23] Auerbach takes Bath as an example of a non-industrial city that gave enthusiastic support to the exhibition.[24]

If there had been doubt about this project coming to fruition, the *SJ* commented in the autumn of 1850 that 'at length the actual work of erecting a building wherein the products of the Industry of All Nations are to be collected has been commenced'.[25] When it was completed the sheer scale was described relative to somewhere more familiar to Salisbury:

> *An approximate estimate may be formed of the immensity of the Crystal Palace by a reference to our own Cathedral; the former being four times the length of the latter (wanting forty feet only) and the transept being double the width of the transept of the Cathedral (wanting two feet only). The height of the roof of the Crystal Palace is less by seventeen feet that that of the nave and the transept of the Cathedral, but the height of the transept of the former exceeds that of the latter by twenty-seven feet.[26]*

The opening of Great Exhibition on 1 May 1851 was reported promptly in the *SJ*.[27] In following weeks there were detailed descriptions of what was to be seen in the Crystal Palace, syndicated from a national newspaper

THE GREAT EXHIBITION ON A CROWDED DAY.

The Illustrated Exhibitor, 1st November, 1851 - The Main Eastern Avenue - From a Photograph by Fehrenbach

source so there is no local context. The *SWH* confirmed that its synopsis was 'abridged from *The Times*'.[28] Readers were taken around the globe with lyrical enthusiasm in the style of a tour guide. Daily attendance figures were published, and in October 1851 it was reported that on one day alone the number of visitors to 'the Crystal Palace on Wednesday was equal to twelve times the population of the city of Salisbury.'[29]

In mid-May it was reported in the *SJ* that 'we have heard of more than one employer in this city who intends treating his workmen to a visit to the Great Exhibition ...'.[30] By the middle of June local businesses in Salisbury were noted in displaying acts of 'spontaneous liberality'. 'The banking firm of Messrs Everett and Smith, of this city, purpose giving their clerks £5 each, and a week's holiday, to enjoy themselves at the Great Exhibition.' [31]

Chaplin, although he had a commercial vested interest, also joined in with the spirit of liberality. In July it was noted that that South-Western Railway Company workers were to get a holiday and free travel to go the Great Exhibition, though arrangements were to be made 'in such a manner that no public inconvenience may be experienced by their absence from duty.'[32]

One of the characteristics of the provincial reaction to the Great

Exhibition was the response of the nobility and landed classes. There was also mention of Lord Radnor 'and some neighbouring landowners' enabling workers from their estates to visit the exhibition.[33]

For the general population, special exhibition trains were run each week from 17 June. Initially these left Salisbury at 8.10 am on a Tuesday and returned at 3.30 pm on a Friday. Return fares were £1 for First Class, 13s 8d (66p) for second, and 7s 7d (36p) for third. Advertisements for a boarding house near Waterloo offered bed and breakfast for 2s 6d (12.5p) and dinner for 1s (5p). This had a dramatic effect on passenger numbers which reached a peak of well over 100,000 in August 1851, falling back to the 'normal' level of about half that after the exhibition closed.[34]

The *Salisbury Journal* kept its readers well informed throughout the lifecycle of the Exhibition; the period of planning, the construction of the Crystal Palace, the Exhibition itself and its aftermath.[35] The national press noted Salisbury's forthcoming involvement in the Great Exhibition. In September 1850 *The Morning Chronicle* noted that the Salisbury Local Committee had applied for allotment of space.[36]

Places within the Crystal Palace were at a premium. According to the Official Catalogue, there were four exhibitors from the Salisbury area allocated space 87 horizontal feet by 4 feet vertical. These were the cutler William Beach, who exhibited in Class 21, Cutlery, Edge and Hand Tools on the North Gallery; Thomas John Holloway, rope manufacturer, who exhibited in Class 14, Flax and Hemp; George Churchill clock maker of Downton, who exhibited in Class X, Horology and Mary Ann Uphill, from Fonthill Bishop, who was an embroiderer, exhibited in Class 19, Tapestry, Carpets, Floor Cloths, Lace and Embroidery.

William Beach was a member of a long-established family of cutlers. In

---

48   BEACH, W., *Salisbury*—**Manufacturer.**

Assortment of cutlery, including fox-pad and fawn's-feet hunting-knives.

Newly designed pearl paper-folding knife, representing the crown, sword, and sceptre, with engraved views of Wilton House, Wilton Church, Salisbury Cathedral, and Stonehenge.

Carvers' pruning knives, shooting knives, &c.

Fine scissors, in newly invented steel cases for chatelaines.   Model of Stonehenge.

Official Descriptive and Illustrated Catalogue of the Great Exhibition 1851, London, 1851, Volume II, 593. Class 21. Cutlery, Edge and Hand Tools. Cat No 48.

1851 he was aged 57, and was living in Catherine Street with his wife, two adult daughters and two sons, one described as a 'clerk in office' and the other following in his father's footsteps as a cutler.[37] Beach was proud of his dominance in this ancient craft. In December 1850 he advertised saying he was employing more workmen, 'being now the only Manufacturer [of cutlery] in the City it is his intention to support the local fame of the Trade by producing the best Description of goods'.[38]

Beach did not get his exhibits to the Crystal Palace in time for the opening, and it was reported that while he had delivered them on 21 May 'the time has now expired for the receipt of goods from English exhibitors; and we understand that the above ['A very superior case of cutlery'] was the last package allowed to be taken in.'[39] Beach also exhibited a model of Stonehenge.

The quality of Beach's work was recognised by the Jury at the Exhibition with the award of an honourable mention. The SJ commented: 'We are glad to learn that the reputation antiently enjoyed by the cutlers of Salisbury did not pass unrepresented or unnoticed among the other industrial products in the Crystal Palace'.[40]

In 1851 Thomas John Holloway lived at the Manor House, Milford. He was aged 31, a rope maker, his wife Jane was 32 and they had three sons aged 5, 3 and 2. There were three female servants in the household. Mr and Mrs Holloway both came from London, Thomas's father was a saddler and harness maker. [41]

The SJ again expressed local pride in his presence at the exhibition, and used the occasion to make a wider point: 'We are happy to learn that the Jury in Class 14 have made honourable mention of the specimens of cordage exhibited by Mr T J Holloway of this city, which were manufactured *exclusively from British flax*. The value of this ... notice on the part of the Jury is enhanced by the circumstances of their being the only specimens manufactured from British flax that were thought worthy of being thus specially distinguished. Exhibiting, as these specimens do, some of the capabilities of flax of home-growth, we congratulate Mr Holloway on the result, and trust it will give an impetus to the cultivation of this important article in our own neighbourhood.[42]

---

74 HOLLOWAY, THOMAS JOHN, *Salisbury*—Manufacturer. Hemp and flax twines.

Official Descriptive and Illustrated Catalogue of the Great Exhibition 1851, London, 1851, Volume II, 515. Class 14. Flax and Hemp. Cat No 74.

Sadly for the Holloways, the business did not prosper, or perhaps Mr Holloway's attention was diverted elsewhere. In August 1854 he was declared bankrupt, and the subsequent enquiries revealed serious debts. Described as someone who had always moved in a most respectable sphere, he was criticised for being dilatory at producing balance sheets of his financial situation, and for attending race meetings while the enquiries were under way. By that time he had five children, and was given a weekly allowance of £5, subsequently reduced to £3. The bankruptcy was annulled in the Spring of 1855.[44]

George Churchill exhibited a 'musical clock'. His name appears on a number of local clocks but it is thought that much of his work was converting and repairing of clocks, rather than manufacture.[45] In 1851 he was a 40 year old widower, described as 'Smith. Journeyman', living in the Borough in Downton. Ten years later he had remarried, and was the innkeeper of the White Horse.[46] A directory of 1865 confirms his residence at the White Horse, but not until 1875 was he described as a watch and clockmaker.

Mary Ann Uphill seems to have been a skilled needlewoman. In the 1841 census James (50, plasterer) and Mary Ann (50, lace maker) Uphill were living in Fonthill Bishop with their son William (25, plasterer). In 1861 there were no Uphills in the village. William had been born in Devon, but while they were in Fonthill Bishop the Uphills had three daughters, and another son who died aged 9 months. At the time of the 1851 census Mary Uphill was staying with her daughter Louisa and son-in-law Joseph Shepherd (a printer compositor) in Marylebone, London. It appears that after James's death in 1854, Mary Ann moved to Shaftesbury where William was working as an 'ornamental plasterer'. She died in 1861, 'abode Shaftesbury'.

There were other exhibits at the Crystal Palace that had a connection with southern Wiltshire. Although Wilton had not provided a Local Committee, there were exhibits from the town.

A 'Rogers of Wilton' exhibited 'Specimens of embroidery – 'Esther and Morecai'' in Class 19 Tapestry, Carpets, Floor Cloths in the South Central Gallery. It has yet to be established that this Rogers was of Wilton in Wiltshire. The 1852 directory for Wilton lists two Rogers in Wilton but neither connected with textiles.

The London architects Wyatt & Brandon of 77 Great Russell Street, Bloomsbury exhibited a 'Model in card (by Mr Stephen Salter, Elvar Cottage, Hammersmith, London) of the new church of St Mary and St Nicholas, at Wilton in the Main Avenue. The church had been built between 1841 and 1844 at a cost of £20,000.

Queen Victoria exhibited an Axminster carpet, designed by Ludwig

323   UPHILL, MARY ANN, *Fonthill Bishop, Salisbury—*
Designer and Manufacturer.

A cushion for the toilet, composed of thread and fine gold twist of different texture. In the centre of this work is introduced the profile of Her Majesty, Prince Albert, and all the Royal Family, with their initials. The band round the work has this motto worked in letters of lace,—"Long live Victoria Queen of England, Prince Albert, and all the Royal Family." The whole work is ornamented with the Crown of England, the Rose and Thistle, Bible and Sceptre, and other emblems of Royalty.

Twist, of different texture, in cushion lace.

A lace scarf, and a bassinette lace cradle-cover of similar manufacture.

Official Descriptive and Illustrated Catalogue of the Great Exhibition 1851, London, 1851, Volume II, 571. Class 19. Tapestry, Carpets, Floor Cloths, Lace and Embroidery. Cat No 323.

Gruner (1801-1882), expressly to the order of Prince Albert for the Green Drawing Room of Windsor Castle, and manufactured in 1850 by Messrs Blackmore Brothers, at Wilton, for the retailer Messrs Watson, Bell & Co.[47] It has been widely claimed that Queen Victoria had commissioned Blackmore to weave her five great masterpieces for Windsor Castle and that all five appeared at the Crystal Palace. Only one carpet by Blackmore Brothers is confirmed by the Official Catalogue as being on display.

Michael O'Connor (1801-1867) and his son Arthur O'Connor (1826-1873) exhibited in Class 24 Glass, in the North-East Gallery, a stained glass memorial lancet which can be seen in the South East transept, East elevation, of Salisbury Cathedral. This window was erected by the officers and survivors of the 62nd (Wiltshire) Regiment of Foot in memory of the officers and men of that regiment who fell during the Sutlej campaign of 1845-1846 in the Punjab.[48]

Richard Cockle Lucas (1800-1883), who had been born in Salisbury, exhibited a number of ivory carvings and imitation bronzes, chiefly of classical subjects, and marble, wax, and ivory medallion portraits that were displayed in the Fine Art Court. Several pieces of his work were subsequently purchased by the National Portrait Gallery.[49]

Benjamin Cheverton, born in Quidhampton in 1794, demonstrated his reducing machine[50] at the Great Exhibition in 1851 and won a gold medal for his copy of 'Theseus' from the Elgin collection in the British Museum.

Section III of Class XXIII. Part of the display of Elkington, Mason & Co. '"Theseus" reduced by Mr Cheverton from the original in the British Museum, made for the Arundel Society. In electro-bronze.' Also, Class XXX Sculpture, Models, 194 'Statuettes, busts, and bas-reliefs, in ivory, alabaster, marble, and metal; carved by a machine from originals of a larger size. Those in ivory and marble, not finished by hand.'

The *Hampshire Advertiser & Salisbury Guardian* noted:

> *Amongst the multifarious native productions exhibited at the Crystal Palace, is a pocket of hops, being a sample of thirteen pockets grown by Mr. Pain, of Fareham, and considered of almost unequalled excellence. As the quality of Salisbury beer deservedly stands high, these hops have been not inappropriately been assigned for that beverage, having been purchased by the proprietors of Maton's brewery, in Milford-street.[51]*

The legacy of the Great Exhibition in Salisbury was primarily to be found in the holding of a local exhibition in 1852.[52] It built on the idea that the totality of a community could be brought together under one roof for the education and delight of visitors. The activities represented there revealed the diversity of the local economy and of the interests to be found in the area. Its title confirms this variety, and the contemporary interpretation of what was desirable in terms of collections: Salisbury Exhibition of Local

**WYATT & BRANDON, 77 *Great Russell Street, Bloomsbury*
—Architects.**
Model in card (by Mr. Stephen Salter, Elvar Cottage, Hammersmith, London) of the new church of St. Mary and St. Nicholas, at Wilton, in the county of Wilts, erected by the Right Honourable Sydney Herbert, M.P., from the design of the exhibitors. The exterior is entirely of stone, and interior decorated with marble, mosaic, and painted glass. It is the first example of the introduction of the Romanesque style of architecture into this country. Its length is 156 feet, the breadth 60 feet, height of nave 54 feet, and of campanile 120 feet.
Model in card of the new assize courts for the county, erected at Cambridge, from the designs of the exhibitors. The exterior of the principal front is of Whitby stone, and the fittings of the interior are of oak. The principal feature of the design is the arcade, which is adopted in preference

Official Descriptive and Illustrated Catalogue of the Great Exhibition 1851, London, 1851, Volume II, p.854. Miscellaneous Objects. Main Avenue.

Salisbury Cathedral, South-east transept. Michael O'Connor and Arthur O'Connor, in memory of the officers and men of the 62nd (Wiltshire) Regiment of Foot who fell during the Sutlej campaign of 1845-1846 in the Punjab. Courtesy of Salisbury Cathedral Stained Glass (photo archive)

Industry, Amateur Productions, Works of Art, Antiquities, Objects of Taste, Articles of Vertu etc'

Both Beach and Holloway exhibited there, and their achievements at the Crystal Palace were credited in the catalogue. Others associated with the Crystal Palace exhibition who contributed to the local event included R C Lucas and C M Lee. Septimus Roe demonstrated an Austrian perfume Fountain Beach ('as in Great Exhibition'). Beach also exhibited at the 1862 International Exhibition in London, in CLASS XXXII, Cutlery and Edge Tools 'Case of assorted cutlery of Salisbury manufacture. This case contains carving, table, sportsmen's, pocket, ditto; razors, daggers, &c. These goods are forged from the pen, pruning, and paper knives; scissors, and cases of best cast-steel, and ground and fitted by the exhibitor'.[53] He continued to mention his success in 1851 in his advertisements.

Quite what triggered the interest in the Great Exhibition amongst the Salisbury population remains unclear. After a cautious beginning, enthusiasm for the major display of the world's productions grew amongst the citizens, and significant numbers of them made the journey from Wiltshire to London to have personal experience of the delights to be found in the Crystal Palace.

Throughout the period of the exhibition, Salisbury's citizens had a number of other concerns which held their attention. In addition to the usual day-to-day reports in the local papers of court proceedings, business developments, tragic accidents, horticultural shows and cricket matches, there were certain critical matters for the city over the period of 1850-51. The cheese market was being rebuilt, taking time and finances of the council.[54] Although Salisbury had gained its first railway line in 1847, this only provided a link to London via Bishopstoke. Debates continued over the construction of a line to the west of Salisbury, and over the provision of a direct route to the capital.[55] Following the cholera epidemic of 1849, Thomas Rammell, an inspector from the Board of Health visited the city in the summer of 1851 and his report would have far reaching consequences for Salisbury.[56] Catholic emancipation was a continuing issue; there was a dramatic 'no-popery' demonstration in the city in November 1850.[57]

At the same time as the Local Committee was soliciting contributions for the Great Exhibition, subscriptions were being collected for memorials to the Dean, Francis Lear, who had died 23 March 1850, and for Dr Brassey Hole who had 'sacrificed his life in his zealous and gratuitous services during the prevalence of the late visitation of cholera'.[58]

But more important than all these was the ongoing debate over Free Trade. The exhibition was interpreted as welcoming overseas products into Britain, that would compete with those made at home. And it was seen as another blow to the prosperity of British agriculture, whose interests were considered to have been destroyed with the repeal of the Corn Laws in 1846. There was a vocal and active lobby in favour of Protection in south Wiltshire, and at the very time the Council was trying to encourage support for the exhibition, a petition to Lord John Russell was collected and a huge 'Protectionist Banquet' held in Salisbury.[59] In practice agriculture was entering a period of prosperity; both sides of the argument exaggerated the significance of repeal, and despite increasing industrialisation, the agricultural

Billhead of William Beach 1869, WSA 2308/45 Theological College, accounts and receipts

sector continued to have political influence.[60] This did not stop the issue taking a great deal of attention away from anything else, particularly in the southern counties.

Salisbury approached the 1851 Great Exhibition with more enthusiasm than some places and less than others. There is perhaps nothing more curious about this than that for many citizens London was considered somewhat remote, with very different priorities.[61] For those who did make the journey to the Crystal Palace it was an overwhelming experience that gave a unique view of the wider world and stayed in the memories of those who visited for decades afterwards.[62]

Bibliography

Official Descriptive and Illustrated Catalogue of the Great Exhibition 1851, London, 1851 (3 volumes)

First Report of the Commissioners for the Exhibition of 1851, London, 1852

Auerbach, Jeffrey A, 1999, *The Great Exhibition of 1851. A Nation on Display,* Yale University Press

Hall, Herbert Byng, 1851, *The West of England and the Exhibition, 1851,* Longman and Co.

Snell, Michael, 1986, *Clocks and Clockmakers of Salisbury,* Hobnob Press

Notes

1   *Salisbury and Winchester Journal* (hereafter *SJ*) 8 September 1849

2   The *SJ* was the oldest Wiltshire newspaper, purchased by James Bennett following the bankruptcy of William Bird Brodie, under whom it had strongly supported the Whigs and parliamentary reform. Under Bennett it returned to 'open to all parties, influenced by none'. Conversely, the *Salisbury & Wiltshire Herald* (hereafter *SWH*) described itself as 'very Conservative', an advocate of the 'interests of agriculture', and attached to the Church of England. *Wiltshire Newspapers: a guide,* 2003, Wiltshire Local History Forum, 7

3   Auerbach, Jeffrey A, 1999, *The Great Exhibition of 1851. A Nation on Display,* Yale University Press, 72-3

4   Hall, Herbert Byng, 1851, *The West of England and the Exhibition, 1851,* Longman and Co, 331-2

5   *SWH* 4 May 1850

6   Auerbach, 1999, 87

7   *The Standard,* Saturday 26 October 1850

8   *SJ* 16 March 1850. The official invitation was 'profusely overlaid in gold and executed in a most finished and elegant manner'.

9   *SJ* 6 April 1850

10 *Hampshire Advertiser & Salisbury Guardian,* Saturday, 15 February 1851

11 *SJ* 4 May 1850

12 Auerbach, 1999, 71

13 He was head of the well-known carriers and coach proprietors, Chaplin & Horne

which in 1840 became carrying agent to the Grand Junction Railway. Chaplin was an influential and well-connected businessman. He was, for instance, a member of the board of the Submarine Telegraph Company that in 1851 was securing a telegraph cable link between England and France.

14 *SJ* 30 January and 22 March 1847

15 WSA G23/100/2 217 Council meeting 20 March 1850

16 Slater's Directory 1852

17 WSA G23/100/2 256

18 *SJ* 27 April 1850

19 *SJ* 4 May 1850. This coincided with protectionist campaign, memorial to Lord John Russell, and huge dinner. See conclusion for indication of other pre-occupations at the time.

20 *SWH* 4 May 1850

21 *SJ* 3 August 1850

22 *SJ* 8 June 1850

23 *SJ* 8 June 1850

24 Auerbach, 1999, 80–81

25 *SJ* 5 Oct 1850

26 *SJ* 17 May 1851

27 *SJ* 3 May 1851

28 *SWH* 10 May 1851

29 *SJ* 11 October 1851. Salisbury had a population of 11, 657 in 1851.

30 *SJ* 17 May 1851

31 *SJ* 14 June 1851 and *Hampshire Advertiser & Salisbury Guardian*, 14 June 1851. The article was titled 'Liberality'.

32 *SJ* 19 July1851

33 *SJ* 28 June 1851

34 Elliott John, 2001, 'Salisbury and the Great Exhibition', unpublished paper presented to Salisbury Civic Society.

35 The role of James Smith (1820-1910), the editor of the *Salisbury and Winchester Journal*, has yet to be fully established.

36 *The Morning Chronicle*, 12 September, 1850

37 Census PRO HO 107/1847f 60

38 SJ 14 Dec 1850

39 *Hampshire Advertiser & Salisbury Guardian*, Saturday, 24 May 24 1851 p 5.

40 *SJ* 1 Nov 1851

41 Baptism 16 July 1819 St John the Evangelist, Westminster

42 *SJ* 25 Oct 1851

43 *SJ* 12 August, 19 August, 23 Sept, 11 Nov 1854, 6 Jan 1855

44 *Spectator* archive online, Commercial Gazette, 17 April 1855

45 Snell, Michael, 1986, *Clocks and Clockmakers of Salisbury,* Hobnob Press, 127-8, 205, 234. His work can be seen in Whiteparish, Coombe Bissett, and Downton churches, in Breamore House and in The White Horse Inn in Downton.

46 Census PRO HO107/1846; PRO RG 9/1314

47 Illustrated in *Illustrated London News* 11 October 1851. See http://www. royalcollection.org.uk/collection/44186/carpet

48 On 21 -22 December 1845 the 62nd Foot fought in the Battle of Ferozeshah. The 62nd Foot suffered heavy casualties, including 18 out of 23 officers and 281 out of 560 other ranks. By the end of the first day of battle, no officers were left to take charge of the regiment. Command of the regiment devolved to its sergeants and non-commissioned officers. In honour of their leadership, 21 December became a regimental anniversary. See http://www.thewardrobe.org.uk/research/regimental-timeline/event/event:706

49 Richards, David, 2008, 'Richard Cockle Lucas 1800-1883 Salisbury's eccentric sculptor', *Sarum Chronicle* 8, 51

50 For making small scale replicas of sculptures http://sculpture.gla.ac.uk/view/person.php?id=msib4_1233326872

51 *Hampshire Advertiser & Salisbury Guardian*, 15 February1851, 5. Reference to this exhibit has yet to be identified within the *Official Catalogue*.

52 Howells, Jane, 2002, 'Salisbury's 1852 'Great Exhibition'', *Sarum Chronicle* 2, 25-34. Via profits from the 1852 event, indirectly the Great Exhibition also contributed to the rebuilding of the Poultry Cross.

53 *The International Exhibition of 1862. The Illustrated Catalogue of the Industrial Department. British Division, Vol. II.*, London p.157 cat. no. 6486

54 WSA G23/100/12

55 Chander J, 1983, *Endless Street*, Hobnob Press, 141. For example see *SJ* 29 November 1851

56 Newman R, and Howells J, 2001, *Salisbury Past*, Philimore, 84; *SJ* 14 June 1851

57 Newman and Howells 2001, p 80; Newman, R, 2006, 'Salisbury in the age of cholera', *Sarum Chronicle* 6,14; *SJ* 23 November 1850

58 *SJ* 28 September 1850

59 *SJ* 22 June 1850

60 Chambers, JD, and Mingay, G E, 1966, *The Agricultural Revolution*, Batsford, 158-9

61 It should be noted that Northy, writing *The Popular History of Old & New Sarum* in 1897, mentions neither the 1851 nor 1852 exhibitions, though he does report the visit of Prince Albert to Stonehenge in 1851. Northy, T J, 1897, 254. See *SJ* 6 August 1851 for the Prince Consort's visit. William Small, writing his *Cherished Memories and Associations* in 1881, also makes no mention of the exhibitions. Howells and Newman (eds), 2011, Wiltshire Record Society Vol 64

62 A reunion of children who had visited the Great Exhibition took place in London as late as 1931, but there is no evidence that any people from Salisbury attended this event.

Premonitions and Promises: a Personal View Twenty-four carvings in Sarum St Martin's North aisle

John Spencer

What follows is more speculative than definitive and uncertainties need to be addressed before any claim can be made of a eureka moment. Nevertheless, the possibility of such a revelation has been on the author's mind since he took his first disinterested look at just one of the corbels at the western end of the north aisle. An attempt will made to involve the reader in this vision, for it could throw light not only on the history of Sarum St Martin but also on the stresses which both plagued and informed popular culture in late 15th century Salisbury. The reader is at liberty to dissent from this vision but only when the counter arguments are supported by chapter and verse.

St Martin's is Salisbury's oldest religious foundation but little of the 11th century original survives. What does survive has been the subject of seven brief histories, but the stone corbels referred to in the present title have been largely overlooked and sometimes dismissed as grotesques.[1] Further, their dating to the early 15th century has so far gone unchallenged.[2] It will be argued here that these modest but intriguing images postdate the marriage of Henry VII and Elizabeth of York (1486). Between 12 and 16 feet above the pavement and mostly smaller than the average human head, they are perhaps best seen with binoculars. Six of these carvings can only be reached from the organ-loft and visitors need to obtain permission before climbing a narrow stairway which is approached through the choir vestry. (fig 2)

Fig. 1. Sarum St Martin from the west, as it may have appeared in the 16th century.

Some have seen these carvings as a review of 15th century fashion.[3] Others have suggested that they represent long-forgotten local worthies or perhaps the various estates to which medieval man felt himself called. But

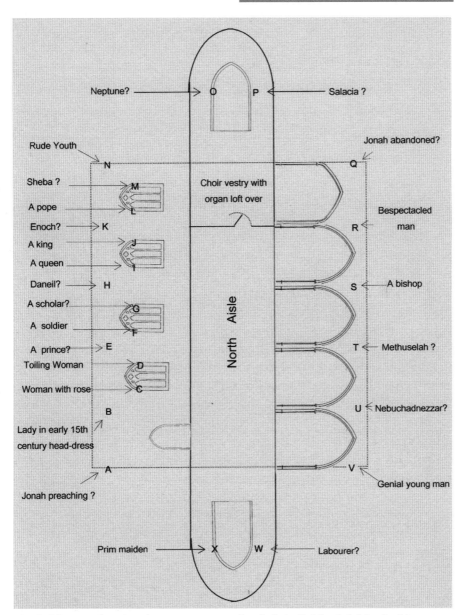

Fig. 2. Diagram showing the arrangement of corbels in St Martin's North aisle.

none of these theories stands up to scrutiny and one may wonder why so many stylistic aspects have been overlooked. Surely most, if not all, of these carvings are quite atypical of what is usually (if sometimes sweepingly) known as The English Gothic?[4] The label-stops which edge the North West

Fig. 3. C Label stop to left of NW window: Woman with rose at her right shoulder.
        © Brian Woodruffe
Fig. 4. D Label stop to right of NW window: Toiling woman
Fig. 5. F Label stop to left of 2nd window: An armed soldier
Fig. 6. G Label stop to right of 2nd window: A scholarly man . © Brian Woodruffe

window C and D, (figs 3, 4) make the point. Here, two stout and un-idealised women face one another. The one on the right is clearly resigned to toil, while the other looks earnestly into the distance. Both have what appear to be attributes, one a rose (often a symbol of meditation)[5] and the other a halter-like collar,[6] suggesting drudgery. As such they seem to represent a contrast between the active and passive lives - a theme which is tied to the most frequently depicted gospel story, that of the Raising of Lazarus, where Mary, unlike her sister, is shown to have 'chosen that good path which shall not be taken away from her'.[7] Where the present images seem exceptional is in their down-to-earth take on humanity – a concern more typical of Flemish art than almost anything produced in England in early centuries. It is as though the sculptor had anticipated something of the earthy humanism found in the paintings of Pieter Bruegel (1525/30-69) and one is obliged to wonder whether the present sculptor was indeed a Fleming or whether a growing interest in Flemish and perhaps Italian art had prompted English craftsmen to broaden their approach.[8]

The corbels F and G, (figs 5, 6) suggest another antitype – that pairing of opposites that brings out otherwise hidden qualities in each. For here a thoughtful and peaceable gentleman is contrasted with a rotund armour-clad foot soldier. The image at G has the air of a credible likeness, rather a rarity at this time, for when speaking likenesses were required the English felt obliged to employ foreigners.[9] It is as though a native delight in caricature, typology and/or poetic idealism got in the way when objectivity was needed.

The carvings at I and J (figs 7, 8) appear to be all typology and no particularity, for here a king and queen seem to be identified as such only

Fig. 7. I Label stop to left of 3rd window: A queen
Fig. 8. J Label stop to right of 3rd window: A king © Brian Woodruffe
Fig. 9. Drawing after a medal in the British Museum (B.M. Reg.1837, 103.24)
depicting Henry VII and Elizabeth of York.
Fig. 10. L Label stop to left of 4th window: A pope

by their crowns and general demeanour. There is little to say who precisely they may represent and existing images show that similar crowns were worn (if somewhat sporadically) by sundry monarchs from the time of Henry II to Henry VII.[10] Perhaps the only telling aspect about these individuals is their bold pairing – putting in mind the celebratory medal struck following the marriage of Henry VII and Elizabeth of York (fig 9), the event most closely associated with the end of the Wars of the Roses. This identification finds support in the carved rose at C where the full-blown naturalistic rendering and the massive stalk (the latter sometimes thought to signify the genetic legitimacy of Henry VII) set the image apart from the highly formal badge associated with the early Tudors.[11] It may also be that the soldier seen at F strengthens this thesis as he could be said to have put up his sword, symbolising peace after strife.

The head at L (fig 10) wears a triple tiara and must surely represent a pope, though the half-hearted manner of its carving might suggest hesitancy about recognising an office that some may have considered contentious. Such concerns about spiritual authority were closely connected to an increasing and popular interest in biblical scholarship,[12] a development which soon turned the minds of the more literate to dark speculation about the end of the world, matters that are hinted at in the next five corbels. But the intended identity of the pope at L cannot be put aside. Looking for a likeness seems even more fruitless than it was for I and J, for the sculptor seems to have resigned himself to a childlike rendering and has simply presented a schematic totem figure. Why, one wonders, that excessively high forehead, those almond eyes and the lugubrious expression? The whole approach is clearly far from the astutely observed head at G and would argue for a

Fig. 11. M Label stop to right of 4th window: A woman in regal costume, possibly the Queen of Sheba

Fig. 12. O Label stop to left of E window: Neptune ?

Fig. 13. P Label stop to right of E window: Salacia ?

Fig. 14. Jonah abandoned to the sea.

different sculptor. Was he perhaps thinking back to Martin V, whose name would certainly fit? Even as one of the youngest popes he had brought an end to the Great Schism (1378-1417) and had reigned in a brief papal golden age before the arrival of two antipopes.[13]

The image at M (fig 11) is female and is also rather crudely carved. To be in keeping with what appears to be an emerging pattern one might expect this elegantly dressed lady to be paired in some way (either as type or antitype?) with the pope and one's mind turns to those whom medieval theologians called Ancestors of Christ. The most obvious subject here would be Sheba, otherwise The Queen of the South, and her association with Solomon. And it is here that premonitions begin, for according to the gospels, Christ compared that Queen's visit to Solomon with his own forthcoming rejection and promised Coming in Judgement.[14]

This evocation of the end of time takes a surprising turn with the next two carved heads at O and P (figs 12, 13). For even after a lengthy search for alternative answers, O can only represent the pagan god, Neptune[15] and P therefore is likely to be his oceanic consort Salacia, the Roman Venus. Together these gods stand for the sea in its various and unpredictable moods. Perhaps it is this reference to a classical theme which has prompted the sculptor to adopt a stylistic shift recalling that development in humanism that drew on the Graeco-Roman imagination.[16] For this enchanting carving of Salacia stands out from all its neighbours as a supreme example of grace and suavity. A hood-like garment encircles her head, starting from the thinnest of forms and gradually widening out with a clockwise sweep, somewhat like a developing wave. Remembering that this carving could be almost contemporary with Botticelli's celebrated 'Birth of Venus' (1484-6),

Fig. 15. Jonah thrown from vessel, carved misericord in Ripon Cathedral, probably by
    William Brounflete. By kind permission of the Chapter of Ripon Cathedral.
Fig. 16. A bracket at NW corner of aisle: Jonah preaching © Brian Woodruffe
Fig. 17. V bracket at SW corner of aisle: Genial young man © Brian Woodruffe
Fig. 18, N Rude Youth. North wall, South East corner. ©Brian Woodruffe

a rational observer might wonder how these or similar perceptions could
travel so well, and, if they did, how they could become entangled with
English Bible-inspired forebodings. Physically closest to the label-stop at P
is the bracket corbel Q (fig 14) and it will be shown that they are linked
thematically, a fact that points towards something in the nature of a common
theme throughout the aisle, whether on label-stops or brackets. The carving
at Q represents an incident in the story of Jonah, whose association with the
unpredictable sea was well known.[17]   But there is yet another link here in
that the carving is located at the eastern end of the church, for theologians
have long associated the prophet's three day ordeal in the belly of a whale
with Christ's death and resurrection, the sacred history that was celebrated
daily either in the adjacent chancel or at a chapel at the end of the aisle. The
inclusion of this note of promise may have been wished on the sculptor
as it clearly taxed his imagination. The problem is that, lacking a suitable
likeness, the colourful Jonah could be recognised only by the inclusion of
some aspect of his story. Here then the sculptor felt obliged to present a
complete and significant scene in the tale. In this case he has chosen the
moment when the prophet, attempting to escape from a sacred duty, met his
comeuppance in a raging sea. The sculptor, less than happy with this task,
seems to have taken his overall arrangement from a pattern book. Some
confirmation of this can be found in a carving in Ripon Cathedral, where a
wood carver may have had access to that same book (fig 15).

However, the Ripon carver clearly understood that the intention of the
design was to show that, in danger of inundation, the sailors had furled their
sails, revealing bare rigging. Sadly, the St Martin's sculptor seems to have
missed the point and to have settled for a meaningless chevron above the

Fig. 19. U bracket South wall, 5th from East: Nebuchadnezzar
Fig. 20. H bracket North wall, 3rd. from East; Daniel? © Brian Woodruffe
Fig. 21.T bracket South wall, 4th from East : Methuselah
Fig. 22. K bracket North wall, 2nd from East : Enoch

prophet's head, a configuration that seems to have left him and subsequent viewers puzzled. But, though failing here, the sculptor's imagination came into its own in the action of the prophet. Jonah seems to be projected forward with an almost baroque twist and presses down on his left leg as if resisting a force from below. His right hand is raised as though preparing to strike something wholly alien, in this case the tempestuous sea. This is the only carving in the entire aisle that could suggest that it had been part of a larger composition, though one other (another three-quarter figure) does launch himself forward at A, (fig 16) and shows the sculptor's interest in dynamic action. The fact that this latter figure presents a scroll (somewhat triumphantly) tends to confirm that this is indeed a second image of the prophet, though this time in the guise of a reformed character.[18] It may be added that the story of Jonah had links to a passage in the Book of Jude, where that apostle refers to the end of time in colourful language: 'Raging waves of the sea, foaming out their own shame.'[19] That imagery will be seen much in line with what has been said about M, O, P & Q. If we suppose that A does indeed represent a second image of Jonah, then the possibility of an overall linking between the bracket and window corbels will have been strengthened. But linking A to Q will also suggest a diametrical pairing (with R linked to B and H to T etc). Perhaps the best way to test this notion is to proceed as though it were true and then review the theory by stages.

Thus, looking along the South East to North West axis, it will be seen that young men at V and N, (figs 17, 18) seem to engage with one another from a distance. A neatly dressed, wholly good natured and smiling youth seems to be encountered by another, offering the rudest of gestures (his stuck-out tongue mirroring the other's goatee). These then may be seen

Fig. 23 B bracket North wall, 5th from East: Lady in early 15th century head-dress
Fig. 24. R bracket South wall, 2nd from East: Bespectacled man
Fig. 25. E bracket North Wall, 4th from East: A prince?
Fig. 26. S bracket South Wall, 3rd from East: A bishop

as two more antitypes strengthening the case for interpreting the bracket carvings diametrically. But before leaving these engaging figures it might be observed that here perhaps is the first sign of comic relief, a theme that will be returned to later.

Following this same pattern would lead the observer to conclude that U and H, (figs 19, 20) should also form some kind of pair, a notion that may be confirmed by reference to the Bible, which, as has been suggested above, was becoming better known.[20] In this case it is Daniel's account of his confrontation with Nebuchadnezzar that has attracted attention.[21] Troubled (and the figure at H certainly looks very introspective if not troubled) by his own prophetic powers,

Daniel finds that his interpretation of Nebuchadnezzar's dream is terribly realised when the mighty king of Babylon is reduced to eat grass like an ox as seems possible at U. With this story in mind the carvings will be seen to fit in place without further comment save to say that it may have been an unthinking glance at U that suggested the word grotesques as a blanket term for all of the carvings in the North aisle.[22]

Two further heads T and K, (figs 21, 22) present a rather similar old/young pairing. Almost lost among the early patriarchs but apparently brimming with near magical powers, the exceedingly long lived Methuselah, T, and the wonderfully favoured Enoch, K, must have appealed to sculptors and parishioners whose lives were often ill-starred and short.[23] Enoch was mostly known from the Book of Jude, where (before the young man's mysterious translation to heaven) he had predicted: 'Behold, the Lord cometh with ten thousand of his saints, to execute judgement upon all…'. [24]

Enoch's supposed grandson, the all but un-ageing Methuselah, has so

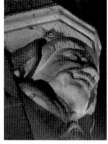

Fig. 27. Corbel in Salisbury Cathedral Library, Bishop Ayscough. © Dr John Crook
Fig. 28. W label stop to left of West window: A labourer?
Fig. 29. X label stop to right of West window: A prim maiden

fascinated the sculptor that he has made the patriarch's beard grow with such energy that one might imagine that, like its owner, it might seem to go on unabated. Surely a *tour de force*? The fact that access to so much apocalyptic literature appears to have been through the book of Jude and other New Testament sources may be understood when one realises that English versions of the Old Testament (being a literal translations of the Vulgate) were hard to read and that hand written copies of Wycliffe's New Testament (which included the Book of Jude) were altogether more accessible by the late fifteenth century.

This trawl through prophetic history seems to stall with the heads at B and R (figs 23, 24). A plaster cast of the bespectacled figure at R has been held by the College of Optometrists for some years, but they doubt the received wisdom that it represents a nun. Further, judging from their comments referred to in note 2, one may wonder whether the College had misgivings about the early date they had been given. Bearing in mind that Salisbury (and, at one time, neighbouring Clarendon) had been the home of many engaged in copying liturgical documents,[25] it seems likely that this figure represents a scribe, in which case the close-fitting cowl and glasses might seem in keeping with that profession. Detailed inspection suggests that the head is that of a young man and his apparent diligence would seem to contrast with the self-absorbed (and diametrically paired) wimpled lady at B, the very image of vanity. Perhaps the artist had to look back half a century to the mores of a less worried past to find a costume that would give his message full force.[26] So these two, B and R may offer yet another antitype. Apart from that, the only thing that unites them is a rigorous and formal handling, a matter which suggests that they are both by the same extraordinary craftsman.

There is another clear shift from biblical typology at E and S (figs 25, 26) for the bishop at S may well have reminded worshipers of Bishop Ayscough, murdered by followers of John Cade in nearby Edington in June 1450. True, the connection with Ayscough is tenuous, for it only rests on the fact that his cope is decorated with a five point design, a feature also seen in a carving known to represent Ayscough and to be found on the inside of the door to the Cathedral Library (fig 27).[27] But such an interpretation leaves the identification of his supposedly paired image at E unanswered, save to say that the amulet at his forehead might indicate access to some kind of occult or worldly wisdom rather than the sacred insight that had been conferred on the Bishop.[28]

Returning to the remaining label-stops: W and X (figs 28, 29) it seems that W is a down-to-earth labourer and X a prim lady who would clearly avoid work if she could. Apart from being antitypes, could these two represent Mr Everyman and his wife, characters witnessing a theatrical performance? For the full blown theatre was yet another of those continental innovations, destined to build on Britain's interest in miracle plays and the like. If these disparate characters are a reminder of the contrast between the active and passive life, as has been suggested with regard to C and D, then here they surely come with laughter attached. How very English. It may even be that their early 15th century costume is a deliberate anachronism. The idea that so many serious concerns are being watched over by frumps could be grounds for amusement.

Conclusions

Despite some variation in subject matter, style and competence there seems to be a cohesion between the above carvings, suggesting either a powerful director or a team of sculptors united by the discipline of work, a wide-ranging interest in the arts and by a common humanity. It is that humanity and the ever widening reach of the arts that seems to have triumphed, for individuality and experiment seems to show itself at every turn.[29]

It is well known that from the time of Wycliffe to the Reformation, England had been subject to serious theological controversy, much of it vigorously suppressed by the ruling orthodoxy and, according to John Capgrave, the most potent aspect of this dissent, Lollardy, 'began first in the diocyse of Salesbury'.[30]

There are several ways in which the fearful and oppressed can, and do, deal with profound existential stress and one of these is to find refuge in the arts.[31] In the 15th century, torn by bickering and, *in extremis*, silenced by the threat of public burnings,[32] some cried out for arbitration and many minds seemed forced to appeal to that most potent of all images, the Last Judgement, a theme suggested by some of the present carvings and in the scores of Doom paintings appearing across the land. It is a searching for other insights, some inspired by the ethos of continental humanism and drawing on classical wisdom, that sets most of the north aisle sculpture apart from so much English Gothic imagery. Having appealed to apocalyptic fears, as ten of the carvings do, some have found the courage to reassess their worries by setting them in a contemporary framework. Others did what those with a stiff upper lip always do. They laughed, much as Chaucer did.

This is a shortened and amended form of a privately printed article given to some of the author's friends. The author is grateful for their comments and suggestions. All photographs by the author unless otherwise stated.

Bibliography

Baker, T H, 1906, *Notes on St Martin's Church and Parish,* Bennett Brothers

Baxter, Philip, 2008, *The Sarum Use, The Ancient Customs of Salisbury,* Spire Books

Benson and Hatcher, 1843, *Old and New Sarum,* 593-5

Brown, Andrew D, 1995, *Popular Piety in Late Medieval England, The Diocese of Salisbury.* Clarendon Press

Chandler, John, 2012, 'The Damned Bishop', *Sarum Chronicle,* 12, 5-18

Crittal, Elizabeth (ed), 1962, *A History of the County of Wiltshire;* Vol 6, 79-81

Cross, Claire, 1999, *Church and People, England 1450-1600,* Blackwell

Cunnington, P and Willet, C. 1969 *Handbook of Medieval Costume,* Faber

Dobson, Barrie, 2010, *The Laity begin to take control, Not Angels, but Anglicans,* Canterbury Press

Fox-Davies, A C, 1928, *A complete Guide to Heraldry,* Bonanza

Gardner, A, 1951, *English Medieval Sculpture,* Cambridge University Press

Hargreaves, H, 1969, *The Wycliffe Versions* in *The Cambridge History of the Bible Vol.2* Cambridge University Press

McKendrick Scot, Lowden John and Doyle Kathleen, 2011, *Royal Manuscripts, The Genius of Illumination.* British Library.

National Association of Decorative and Fine Art Societies, 1988, Record of St Martin's Church Furnishings, Section 200 (hereafter NADFAS)

Pevsner, N, 1955, *The Englishness of English Art,* Penguin

Pevsner, N and Cherry, B, 1975, *The Buildings of England, Wiltshire,* 438f.

Royal Commission on Historical Monuments in England, 1980, *Ancient and Historical Monuments in the City of Salisbury',* I, liv, 32-36, HMSO (hereafter RCHM).

Rouse, Clive, 2004, *Medieval Wall Painting,* Shire Publications

Shortt, H de S, 1950, *St Martin's Church, Salisbury,* Bennett Bros.

Stone, L, 1955, *Sculpture in Britain: The Middle Ages,* Penguin

Notes

1. Baker, 93, RCHM, 33
2. Shortt, 4, Baker, 93 suggests 1430 – 1440. A letter from The College of Optometrists dated 2nd April 2008, refers to earlier correspondence with St Martin's Church Office. It seems that the College had been told that one of the corbels (R: the figure with eyeglasses) 'was believed to date from approximately 1430-1440, but possibly up to 100 years earlier'. The College asked to be informed 'in the event of any archaeological re-assessment of the date as … it is such an important piece of early evidence.'
3. NADFAS, 201, Shortt, 7
4. Pevsner, 1955, 39-45
5. Cirlot, J E, 1976 *A Dictionary of Symbols*, Routledge & Kegan Paul, 60, 193, 371. Fox-Davies, 60,193, 371. It would be interesting to know whether this rose had ever been painted in red and white in the manner of the conjoined symbols of the houses of York and Lancaster. Sadly the image has been given yet another coat of paint (Nov 2013) and there has been no report concerning any underpainting.
6. Neither the Costume Department of the V&A, Reading University Museum of Rural Crafts nor The Weald and Downland Museum have been able to identify this strange feature. Pieter Bruegel's 'Hunters in the Snow' c.1565 (Vienna, Kunsthistorisches Museum) shows a peasant woman pulling another across a frozen pond. However there is no indication that a halter is involved.
7. Luke 10:38ff. Mary & Martha's story is closely tied to that of the Raising of Lazarus – one of the few miracles regularly depicted in English wall painting (Rouse, 44). Perhaps the best know local depiction of this story (featuring strongly contrasted characterisations of Mary & Martha) is a 12th century carving in Chichester Cathedral. Stone, 65
8. McKendrick, Lowden, Doyle. The authors list 154 Royal MSS, of which about one third were produced in the 15th century, mostly in the Netherlands or France
9. See for example Torrigiano's (1472-1528) terracotta portrait bust of Henry VII, in the V&A.
10. Fox-Davies, 356 f. Crowns matching that at J appear to be worn by Henry VII in a corbel in Salisbury Cathedral Library and in St Mary, Fairford (Window 15, below transom 1). Though images of Henry usually show him beardless, this feature can hardly be diagnostic; perhaps the sculptor had virility in mind.
11. Fox-Davies, 269. Stone, 87, 229. Stone discusses a carved rose in King's College Chapel, Cambridge (1512-13) and it will be seen to have something in common with the fleshy rose at C.
12. Brown, 208; Dobson, 113
13. Kelly, J N and Walsh M J, 2010, *Oxford Dictionary of Popes*, Oxford University Press, 239ff.
14. Matt 12:42 : 'The queen of the south shall rise up in judgement with this generation, and shall condemn it: for she came from the uttermost parts of the earth to hear the wisdom of Solomon, and behold a greater than Solomon is here' Images of Sheba (as a so-called 'Ancestor of Christ') are surprisingly common in medieval art. See for example Säuerlander, W, 1970, *Gothic Sculpture in France, 1140-127t.* – where fifteen relevant carvings are discussed. Sheba is also found in English art as in sculpture

at Rochester Cathedral, in stained glass of Canterbury Cathedral and St Mary, Fairford

15 The rather shallow carving at O may well have been based on a late antique *repoussé* (similar perhaps to the mythological oceanic figures that disport themselves on silverware associated with the Projecta Casket (British Museum, Catalogue of Early Christian Antiquities, No. 304). The image is certainly very different in style to the remaining 23 corbels, suggesting that the sculptor had looked far and wide for a suitable model.

16 Such an association with classicism developed remarkably early in Italy, as can be seen, for example, in the pioneering work of Nicolo Pisano (c.1245/50-1284)

17 The typology connected with Jonah seems to have been understood from Early Christians times. See for example a 4th century painting in the Catacomb of Jordani, Rome. Also Stevenson, J, 1978 *The Catacombs: Rediscovered monuments of early Christianity,* Thames and Hudson, 37, 75f.

18 At first sight the prophet seems to be wearing a crown – something that does not feature in Jonah, 4:5f. However, having now seen the carving from above, it appears that this curious device is meant to represent the shade from the burning sun. Perhaps a depiction of the gourd which (according to the story provided the merciful shadow) was just too difficult to fit in such a narrow block of stone?

19 Jude v.14

20 Hargreaves, 18, 338, 410

21 Da 4:18f. Increasing numbers of readers of Wycliffe's New Testament would have already been familiar with Daniel's dark forebodings as set out in Mat 24:15 and Mark 13:14.

22 Baker, 93: 'The North Aisle ... grotesque heads carved on corbels'

23 Gen. 5:21f,

24 Jude v 13

25 Baxter, 44f

26 One may wonder whether it was the identification of this fashion (several similar headdress appear in *Les Très Riches Heures du Duc de Berry* of 1411-16) that prompted Shortt and others to propose an early 15th century dating for the entire north aisle.

27 There are at least 20 carved images of bishops to be seen at ground level in Salisbury Cathedral, but none of their vestments appears to display this five point pattern,

28 The head at B certainly looks princely and perhaps worldly but so far has been difficult to place. It has the air of a true likeness and perhaps a late 15th century viewer would have needed no iconographical clues to identify him.

29 Pevsner (1995), 92 discusses the way schemes in English carving are more standardised and repetitive than contemporary European examples. This is another reason for taking the present scheme of carvings to be continentally inspired.

30 Brown, 202. However, in questioning Capgrave's statement (208) Brown refers to 'a line between orthodoxy and heresy being a shifting no man's land of opinions that were not always easily definable as heretical.'

31 Some anthropologists, psychologists and art historians would see this less about taking refuge (in the sense of hiding) and more about finding strength in the collective unconscious . Less contentiously others would invoke the healing power of art.

32 Chandler, 2012, 13

Recent publications

Chalk & Cheese: Wiltshire's rocks and their impact on the natural and cultural landscapes
Steve Hannath 2014 Ex Libris Press 92pp £7.50
ISBN 978-1-906641-65-8

Steve Hannath's latest book introduces and considers the hugely varied geology of the county and the many ways in which it impacts on its character and history. Copiously illustrated and drawn from a wide range of sources, there are chapters explaining the physical formation of the landscape and rock types, the water table and spring lines, and how together these define variations in agriculture and vegetation; extractive industries, the distribution and use of local materials for buildings; and the locations of settlements. The Chalk & Cheese of the title refer to the contrasting chalk downland of sheep and corn and the clay vales where dairy farming is prevalent.

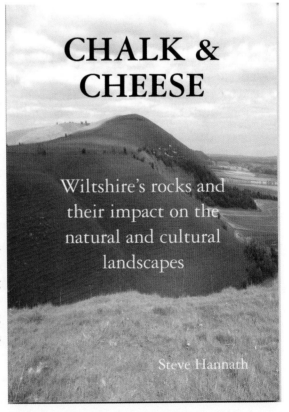

★★★

Music at Midnight: the life and poetry of George Herbert
John Drury 2013 Allen Lane 396 pp £25.00
ISBN 978-1-846-14248-2

John Drury, chaplain of All Souls College Oxford provides a sensitive guide to both George Herbert's short life and his poetry. Herbert was born in 1593 and after a distinguished academic career he entered the priesthood becoming rector of Bemerton in 1629, dying in his parsonage in 1633 just before his fortieth birthday. This book, about someone described as the greatest devotional poet in the English language, has been widely praised. One reviewer simply states that 'it is hard to imagine a better book for anyone ... newly embarking on Herbert'.

Two books have recently been published on Salisbury schools:

Leehurst Swan School: a centenary history
Jane Howells 2013 Shire Publications 64pp £7.99
ISBN 978-0-74781-304-0

A concise and well written account describing the complicated history of the school in Campbell Road. Founded in 1914 as a Catholic convent for girls (Leehurst), it was taken over by the Sisters of La Retraite in 1953. A seemingly revolutionary step was taken in 1996 when the school merged with the local Swan School for Boys and has since thrived as a co-educational independent school taking the name Leehurst Swan in 2007. Changes in education and social history over the hundred years are particularly well documented.

★★★

BWS: the second Sixty Years, through the eyes of those who were there: Reflections on life at Bishop Wordsworth's School in Salisbury, Post War to the New Millennium
Martin Holloway 2014 The Old Wordsworthians Association 192pp £9.99
ISBN 978-0-9928246-0-0

Largely a series of often amusing anecdotes and memories reflecting school life in the Boys' Grammar School in the Close over 'the last six decades'. These include recollections of William Golding who taught English at the school, and former pupil, Ralph Fiennes.

★★★

Life in an English Village: an Economic and Historical survey of the Parish of Corsley in Wiltshire

Maud F Davies, edited with an introductory essay by Jane Howells: first published 1909, new edition with introduction 2013

The Hobnob Press 317pp £12.95 ISBN978-1-906978-05-1

First published in 1909 Maud Davies' *Life in an English Village* was regarded as a groundbreaking, sociological study of the small Wiltshire village of Corsley near Warminster. The publication caused outrage because the 'anonymous' villagers were easily recognised; Maud was accused of 'slandering the poor' and attempts were made to suppress the book. Just four years later Maud died tragically on a London railway line. The new edition includes a detailed introduction by Jane Howells about the author's life and continuing importance, and the mysteries surrounding her premature death.

★★★

Ashcombe, the story of a fifteen year lease

Cecil Beaton, first published 1949; new edition with foreword by Hugo Vickers 2014

The Dovecote Press 124pp £8.00 ISBN 978-0-9573119-8-5

The story of Beaton's love for his remote house Ashcombe, on Cranborne Chase. When he first saw the house, with Edith Olivier and Rex Whistler in 1930, he stated that 'my reaction was instantaneous. It was love at first sight, and from the moment that I stood under the archway, I knew that this place was destined to be mine'.

Beaton's transformation of the house in the 1930s and his growing reputation meant that the great and the scandalous flocked to Ashcombe to savour the extravagant lifestyle offered. The fifteen year lease was not renewed in 1945 and Hugo Vickers writes that Beaton never recovered from its loss.

Andrew Minting and Ruth Newman

Author Biographies

- David Algar has been involved with the archaeology and history of the Salisbury area since the 1950s, writing particularly on numismatics and local ceramics.

- Dr Lucille H Campey is a historian and author of ten books on British emigration to Canada. She is Programme Secretary of the Dinton Historical Society.

- John Chandler is currently Gloucestershire editor of the Victoria County History, but has researched and published extensively on the history of places in Wiltshire and Dorset, especially the Salisbury area. He was formerly general editor of the Wiltshire Record Society and joint editor of *Wiltshire Studies.*

- John Elliott is an architectural historian who used to teach at the University of Reading and the University of London, Royal Holloway and Bedford New College. He is now retired and lives near Salisbury.

- Anthony Hamber, a native of Salisbury, is an independent photographic historian. He has previously published a biography of William Blackmore, *Collecting the American West. The Rise and Fall of William Blackmore,* Hobnob Press, 2010. He is currently completing a major study of the impact of photography at the 1851 Great Exhibition.

- Jane Howells is editor of *Local History News* for the British Association for Local History. She has written a new introduction to the 2013 reprint of Maud Davies's *Life in an English Village.* With Ruth Newman she recently transcribed and edited William Small's *Cherished Memories and Associations* for the Wiltshire Record Society (2011). They are also the authors of *Women in Salisbury Cathedral Close,* Sarum Studies 5, 2014.

- Sue Johnson is a local historian with a special interest in early Victorian Salisbury.

- Ruth Newman is the co-author with Jane Howells of *Salisbury Past,* and in 2011 they edited and transcribed William Small's *Cherished Memories and Associations* for the Wiltshire Record Society. They have recently written *Women in Salisbury Cathedral Close,* Sarum Studies 5, 2014.

Author Biographies

- David Richards is a retired dental surgeon who is now a Blue Badge guide with a particular interest in the history of the people and buildings of the Salisbury area.

- Peter Saunders is Curator Emeritus, formerly Director, of Salisbury Museum. He edited the four-volume *Salisbury Museum Medieval Catalogue* and has published widely on archaeological and museum subjects

- John Spencer was trained as an artist and continues to paint. Meanwhile, specialising in art history, he has taught widely and lectured for the extra-mural departments of the Universities of London, Reading and Oxford. With wide-ranging interests, his principal study has been in the Early Medieval period. A relative newcomer to Salisbury, he is a member of Sarum St Martin's PCC.

- Tim Tatton-Brown is a freelance archaeologist and architectural historian, with a particular interest in ecclesiastical buildings. He is consultant archaeologist to St George's Chapel, Windsor, and to Westminster School and Lambeth Palace.

Women in Salisbury Cathedral Close

Sarum Studies 5

Jane Howells
Ruth Newman

Women in Salisbury Cathedral Close
Sarum Studies 5

Jane Howells and Ruth Newman

ISSN: 1475-1844   ISBN: 978-0-9571692-4-1   240 x 168 mm   96pp   Softback

This book is the first study of women who were connected with the Close. Women have had an influential part in the history of that special place, shaping the social context from its very beginnings in the 13th century.

Some, like Barbara Townsend and Edith Olivier might be familiar, but others will be new to readers – women like the delightful Elizabeth Harris from Malmesbury House or novelist Sarah Fielding, overshadowed by her more famous brother. A group of enterprising Victorian women including Henrietta Lear, Jane Weigall and Annie Moberly influenced the lives of others without upsetting the *status quo*. They lived in the grandest houses and some of the smallest, individually as widows or spinsters, or as part of large families. Details of these residents and others throw light on the diverse ways they contributed to society in the Close over many centuries.

Institutions in the Close have also been important: the Matrons' College and the little known female penitentiary, numerous girls' schools, the Choir School, the Diocesan Training College and girls attending Bishop Wordsworth's School.

The acceptance of women has been of great historical significance and in 2014 there is no longer a feeling of the Close being a community of men.

As the Rev Dame Sarah Mullally (Canon Treasurer of Salisbury Cathedral) writes in her foreword

> *We know that women have always been present in the Cathedral and Close but history does not always record that and so this book plays an important role in reminding us that this was and is the case.*

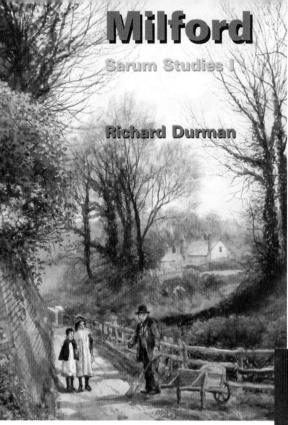

Sarum Studies

This series of small books, produced under the aegis of the *Sarum Chronicle* editorial team, is designed to offer succinct, scholarly and accessible local history publications focusing on the suburbs of Salisbury, or on a particular aspect of the area in the past.

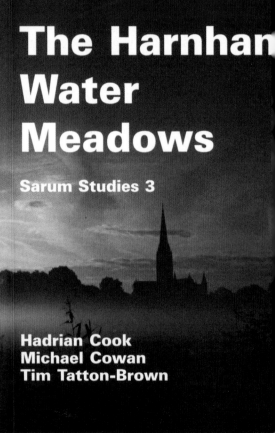

There are now five titles in the list. If you, or someone you know, has research material that might be appropriately published as another Sarum Studies volume, please do get in touch with us.

Sarum Studies 1
Milford by Richard Durman
(2007)

Sarum Studies 2
Harnham Mill by Michael Cowan (2008)

Sarum Studies 3
The Harnham Water Meadows by Hadrian Cook, Michael Cowan and Tim Tatton-Brown (2008)

Harnham Mill
SALISBURY
Sarum Studies 2

Michael Cowan

The oldest surviving paper mill in the country

Harnham
Historical Miscellany

Sarum Studies 4

Edited by Jane Howells

Sarum Studies 4
Harnham Historical Miscellany edited by Jane Howells (2013)

Sarum Studies 5
Women in Salisbury Cathedral Close by Jane Howells and Ruth Newman (2014)